MASTERFUL
LIVING

NEW VOCABULARY FOR THE HOLY LIFE

KEVIN MANNOIA

Visit www.HolinessAndUnity.org.

Masterful Living: New Vocabulary for the Holy Life
Copyright © 2011 by Kevin Mannoia. All rights reserved.
ISBN: 978-0-9831729-2-5

A joint publication of Metaformation, Inc., Ventura, California, and WHC
Publications, Glendora, California.

Design: Lamp Post Inc.
Editor: Anita K. Palmer

MASTERFUL LIVING

NEW VOCABULARY FOR THE HOLY LIFE

KEVIN **MANNOIA**

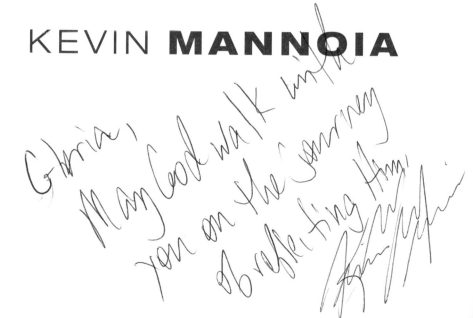

Table **of Contents**

ACKNOWLEDGEMENTS ....*vii*

PROLOGUE.. *ix*

INTRODUCTION ....*xiii*

CHAPTER ONE | *Transformed Character*...*1*

CHAPTER TWO | *Responsible Engagement* *13*

CHAPTER THREE | *Healthy Relationships*..*20*

CHAPTER FOUR | *Wise Decisions* *30*

CHAPTER FIVE | *Integrated Life*.. *40*

CHAPTER SIX | *Purposeful Hearts*...*50*

CHAPTER SEVEN | *Servant Leadership*...*57*

CHAPTER EIGHT | *Meaningful Work*..*69*

CHAPTER NINE | *Curious Thinking*..*82*

CHAPTER TEN | *Restored Self*...*92*

CONCLUSION..*103*

END NOTES *106*

RESOURCES...*109*

ABOUT THE AUTHOR..*110*

ACKNOWLEDGEMENTS

THERE IS NO WAY TO DETERMINE WHEN THE IDEA FOR THIS book actually began. Because more than any other this project represents the nature and passion of my own life, it spans a lifetime—of learning, of growing, of listening and mostly of being formed on the way of Jesus. Because of that, the list of those who have contributed to the ideas is as long as my own existence. But obviously I cannot—and I won't even try to—list all those who have touched my life in forming me.

Chief among those that I do want to name are my own parents whose passion for God and healthy walk with Christ modeled what it means to be wholly saturated with God's character. They forged within me a foundation that allowed experiences and new learning to become allies which I was willing to embrace.

Certainly my wife and family are vital to my thinking as well. Kathy's grace and patience, coupled with guileless intention, remain a constant point of accountability and model of holiness. And I honestly can say that my children have taught me more about the motivating heart of love that God has for His children than my whole educational career combined. I daily am amazed at new insights of love for my children which help me understand God's disposition toward me.

Though I cannot begin to name them all, the denominational leaders at a national and regional level in the WHC across the country have helped me to think creatively in bringing new word sets to the surface. I thank them. And the pastors on whom I have experimented with concepts, ideas, terminology and phrases, thank you.

Inspiring conversations with George Barna, who keeps asking, prodding, and pulling for greater clarity within my own thinking, have been deeply helpful. Always helping me connect it to reality.

Although it may sound trite or super spiritual, I cannot go long in any discussion about this book without expressing deep humility and overwhelming thanks to God for grace, forgiveness, wholeness, and affirmation. I have never felt more intimate with the Lord than while struggling to craft exactly the right phrases in these ten descriptors. The Spirit's gentle nudge or consuming insight have been nothing short of exhilarating. Each day I give thanks to God for salvation—the path of becoming like Jesus. I walk in deeper mourning and joy, insecurity and confidence, weakness and strength than ever before.

"Come, O holy Jesus, to our hearts this day;
Find welcome and place for the fullness of your glory;
Weave us in the mercy of your love,
that we may reflect the light of your gift.

May our hearts be soft to the gentle touch of holiness;
Mold us as the children of your creation;
Use us as the vessels of your love,
that grace and peace will be our name,
written by the inscription of your hand."

Kevin Mannoia
January 2011

PROLOGUE

THEY WALKED HAND IN HAND, FATHER AND YOUNG DAUGHTER, through the grand square in front of St. Peter's Cathedral. This was the Vatican. They had enjoyed the beauty and energy of history flowing throughout the great city of Rome. Now they approached what they both expected would be a highlight of their visit.

Winding their way through the halls of the great structure, they followed the tour group and finally stepped through an inauspicious door which reverently ushered them into a rather small but high ceiling chapel. A hush fell as every head turned upward.

Here they were in the Sistine Chapel. No one needed to say anything. Everybody knew it was the ceiling that drew visitors from around the world. It was one of the important sights the two had wanted to see. Now here they were—standing under the greatest work of art they could imagine.

Heads upturned, they found a place in the middle of the chapel. "Look at the hues," the father whispered to his daughter. "Notice the shape of the figures. See the strokes and complexity of the whole piece."

He wanted his daughter to appreciate good art. And what better place to do it than in this place, under this work. "See the look on the man's face. Notice the reach of God's hand." The father was focused completely, fueled by his daughter's rapt attention. By his words, he invited her to see all the details of the work he had studied in anticipation of this visit. Then he ran out of descriptors; he came to an end of his pointers. Now it was just silence—the end of noise. Reflection. Letting the images do their work. And inner stirrings that were inexplicable.

Then she voiced a quiet question.

"What kind of person was this artist to have created such a work?"

Unpretentious and not expecting any real answer, the daughter voiced the natural question that came to her. In stunned stillness, the father knew in that moment that she had captured the genius of this masterpiece.

She had witnessed the work. She had appreciated the artistry. She had seen the detail and considered the colors and strokes. She had looked at the art, and seen the artist. In that moment, the father knew the art had done its work. It had invited the curiosity of his daughter to see the artist in the work of his hand. She got it.

What kind of person indeed would pour himself into such work? What kind of personality did this work reveal? How did this art reflect the nature of its creator? In her simple question the father knew was the clue to understanding masterful art. It wasn't the delicate features of the product. It wasn't the nuances of the colors. It wasn't the details of the strokes. All that was wonderful. But that was the outcome.

What made this piece truly masterful was the way it opened a window into the nature and personality of the artist. No. Not even that was sufficient, for in stating it that way, the father was still focused on the art. What made this piece truly masterful was the way the personhood of the artist was present in the art. It reflected someone whose life was poured out in its colors and shapes. It was full of that person. It was an extension of the creator for those who had eyes to see. And his daughter had eyes to see.

The pair moved with the crowd to the other end of the chapel.

With a last glance, the father took in the whole ceiling with new appreciation. His focus was turned from the art itself to the nature of the one behind the art. In his daughter's question, the father found with new humility the key that made this a masterpiece. Not simply because it was good, but because it was full of the master who had created it out of his overflowing life. That was truly masterful.

And the father thought of the image above him—God reaching to touch His creation; and a human striving to touch his Creator. Into that humanity God had poured Himself as a crowning creation. His creatures bore His image; reflected His nature; revealed His wholeness. Though marred, their capacity to reflect the Creator remained.

The father knew God could bring alive again the vibrant reflection of His nature in any human who yearned for that touch— reaching to once again reflect the nature of the Master. Longing once again to be full of the Master—and be whole. That was Masterful.

INTRODUCTION

THE WOODEN GATE THAT LED INTO THE PLAY AREA ON THE SIDE of the house was six feet high. To secure it against the wind, the gate had a latch at the bottom, about a foot off the ground and another at the top.

The lower latch was no problem for our children to open. It was easy to reach. The upper latch, however, was another matter. Only our oldest was tall enough to open the gate to get her bike out. The boys weren't even close. Every time they wanted to ride bikes or let friends come in the side yard they had to ask their big sister, or one of us, to unlatch the top latch. It frustrated the little guys when they had to always find one of us to open the gate and let them out to play.

Finally, I decided to do something about it. I tied a string through the eyehole of the top latch and let it hang down low enough for the boys to reach. I'd seen it on dozens of other gates. And it worked. The string put the upper latch within easy reach. They were able to open the gate whenever they wanted without having to ask for help.

Holiness has become like a top latch—just out of reach and hard to understand in ways that really make a difference, or at least make sense. People have left it to the scholars and pastors to understand. Whenever there was any need, they were the ones who had to reach up and unlatch the gate of understanding holiness for real living. Its fullness never seemed to be within easy reach.

Not that it's such a complex idea. It really isn't. But because it has been so warped or misunderstood, we stopped trying to understand it. In the process the richness of its meaning became a shallow, generic platitude that meant whatever folks wanted it to be. Admittedly, it always referred to something that was spiritual. And usually it implied behaviors that were restrictive—as if somehow not doing certain things would help you to achieve a super-spiritual holy state. But being holy is more than looking holy.

What Is Masterful Living?

IN REALITY, HOLINESS IS NOTHING MORE THAN LIVING FULL OF the Master who is holy. It's *Masterful Living*.

In trying to manage our lives, we have missed the deep meaning and transforming fullness that is at the core of masterful living. Trying to find meaning and wholeness in life has become an exercise in balancing the many components of our lives by trying to give them equal time, energy, and importance. Someone writes a book about staying spiritually accountable, another about quiet time, another about how to treat others, and still another about getting your life in order. Frankly, it's exhausting to keep it all balanced.

We've compartmentalized ourselves into components that are like silos, each separately vying for center stage on the journey of living—spiritual, emotional, intellectual, social, to say nothing of our inner being balanced against our outward actions.

But masterful living, in reality, is very simple. It is the convening center that begins with the Master and extends outward through your life. It creates healing and wholeness in a way that integrates who you are inside with what you do in your behavior.

And who better to provide that center than God, whose very nature is holiness. God is the Master who becomes visible in you.

Being masterful is not a matter of imposing a special set of behaviors with a high level of skill. A highly disciplined life is no more masterful apart from the Master than the Sistine Chapel is masterful apart from the artist.

Rather, masterful living is a condition that represents a greater element of God in you. So, as God is one (complete), you also become one—complete and whole in Him despite our culture's divided and subdivided lifestyle. You become healed from the effects of God's vacancy from your life. And since holiness is so much a part of God's very nature, wholeness and healing come when we allow ourselves to simply reflect God's image in us.

This book has a simple mission—to invite you to appropriate masterful living into your life by putting it within easy reach.

The Richness of Ambiguity

HOLINESS IS PERHAPS ONE OF THE MOST MISUNDERSTOOD themes in a Christian's daily walk. Yet it appears in the Scriptures more often than most other great themes. We spend a lot of time discussing and studying grand ideas like the atonement, mercy, salvation, judgment, grace—and these are amazing demonstrations of God's engagement with us. But for the most part they represent God's actions toward us. He is "doing" something in response to our fallenness. For example, the atonement describes God satisfying the cost of human sin; mercy is God's patience with our offense; and justice is God's way of dealing with disparity.

Holiness is different. Although it motivates God's action toward us, it is part and parcel to the nature of who God is. It is God's very essence, nature, identity—not merely an action. That makes a big difference in how we understand it and appropriate it in our lives. We can hardly expect to know God without being affected by God's holiness.

As we look through Scripture, every time the idea or a related concept is mentioned it seems as though the meaning is different and a different word is used. At times God wants people to sanctify themselves—which is the process of becoming holy. Other times, people are told to sanctify objects or animals. Often the agent is God or God's Spirit. At other times it is people, or even places.

Holy, holiness, sanctification, purified, set apart, perfected—these terms all convey some dimension of this great theme in Scripture that attempts to show God's holiness. In the different words we attempt to find commonality. In fact it is this diversity of reference and lack of clarity that perhaps best conveys the power of holiness for us.

You may think I'm crazy to say that the lack of clarity is a good thing. But that's exactly what I mean. Since holiness describes God's nature, not just God's actions toward us, I would be worried if we *could* describe it clearly. That would mean God is pretty small. Since masterful living means living a life that is full of the Master, who is by nature holy, it is larger than our ability to parse, dissect, analyze, and contain. And that's what makes it so exciting to pursue, and so powerful in transforming our daily living.

Three Dimensions

MASTERFUL LIVING IS RELATIONAL MORE THAN PROPOSITIONAL. It cannot be reduced to a formula. Nor is it merely a doctrine that can be acquired by study or to which we give mental assent. That would be like admiring the artwork without acknowledging the artist—placing more importance on the masterpiece than on the master. Rather, it begins in God's nature and overflows in a transforming relationship. And that transformation is not limited to a person or a group of people. It includes all of what God first made whole.

Masterful living is descriptive more than prescriptive. It is not an elixir that we take to fix all the woes of our broken condition. You cannot practice masterful living by simply conforming to predetermined rules or behavioral expectations—whether established by your own hopes or by some organized effort to create moral codes. It is not achieved by applying a prescribed formula.

Rather, masterful living is a result of willingly letting the Master, who is holy, be seen through the nature and priorities of your daily life. Of course, the important word there is "willingly." Giving up control in determining the nature of your life and what's important to you is a big step of release and vulnerability. It's an act of the will—a choice you make. It is the evidence of living full of the Master.

Masterful living is centered more than bounded. It does not draw a circle around a range of behaviors or beliefs that are permissible and then adopt a fortress mentality against any threat to the boundary. Rather than fear of contamination from foreign thinking, masterful living welcomes it into the range of its influence. It is centered in deep, relational knowledge of God's holy nature. From that secure, centered place, daily living takes on freedom to explore outwardly and influence the choices that you make every day. It is not cloistered and protectionist, it is generous and influential. It is not inwardly focused, but outwardly expansionistic.

So what might a person look like who walks the journey of living full of the Master? What are the descriptors of one who pursues holiness? What are the outcomes that give evidence of a life that is shaped by God's holy nature? What may be a living picture that reflects the holy Master? Not that these outcomes should become the object to be sought after; they are a result, descriptors, visible evidence of a holy Master vibrantly shaping your life into the reflection of His holy nature. Living full of the Master transforms your nature in becoming holy as God is holy. It reorders your priorities—making God's priorities your priorities.

That is masterful living.

Chapter **One**

TRANSFORMED CHARACTER

BEAM ME UP, SCOTTIE."

Remember *Star Trek* and the famous transporter room on the Starship Enterprise? Turns out that Captain Kirk never actually uttered those exact four words on the television series that aired in the late 1960s, and Engineer Scott seldom ran the transporter himself. But the phrase has made its way into our culture nonetheless. At Kirk's command, Scottie would move the transporter slides with the precision of a surgeon and Kirk would materialize from his away mission on some distant planet. In the process, his body was "dematerialized," transported through miles of space, and "rematerialized" safely in the transporter room of his spaceship.

You've probably grown so accustomed to the idea of transportation that you haven't thought much about what the very word implies. The Transportation Security Agency is ever present in airports. Public transportation is a must for anyone in an urban setting. Look at the sides of most semi-trucks on the highway. The word describes their basic function of moving material from one place to another.

The idea of transportation implies two or more locations. There is a starting place and a destination. The part of the word that gives it away is *trans*, which means above or beyond, and implies more than one. In transporting something you are moving it from one location to another. So transportation deals with multiple locations.

In similar fashion, the idea of *transformation* implies multiples. Only in this case it's not multiple locations, but multiple conditions. We transform something when we change it from one condition to another. It happens either gradually or quickly. Something is made again, or in some way made different when we transform it.

You transform your body when you go on a diet—from fat to thin. You transform your image when you change your hairdo or wardrobe—from casual to stylish. You transform your work environment when you establish new expectations or procedures—from bossy to empowering.

In every case of transformation two things are present: The possibility of options, and the power to choose. You cannot transform something from one condition to the same condition any more than you can transport something without moving it. That's stagnancy. For transformation really to happen, a new or different condition must be a possibility. And since there are multiple conditions available, you have the ability to choose which condition will be yours.

When we talk about transformed character, then, keep those factors in mind. It means that you have a choice among multiple options of conditions that will be yours. Masterful living means that you make the choice to let the condition of your life characterize the Master who fills you. In pursuing holiness, the Master is God who is perfectly embodied in Jesus. And so God's nature of holiness is the condition that begins to be seen as your nature is transformed. It looks like Christ.

When you are full of the Master, the transformation will be a natural consequence. It's not that you shop for a life condition like you shop for a new car, picking the options and characteristics you want. You make a choice regarding what master will be your reference point. What master will you let fill you and influence you? Once that choice is made, your life will begin to take on the characteristics of that master. Over time with each circumstance along your way, you will become more and more like the Master in you. And in that, you are being transformed into a new condition. A condition which is characteristic of the one who fills you.

So one of the most important questions you can ask yourself is this: *Who's your master?*

The answer will determine the kind of life you will lead, since the master shapes the life of the servant. If your master is money—you will become greedy. If your master is power—you will become abusive. If your master is position—you will become manipulative. If your master is self—you will become egotistical. If your master is God—you will become Christ-like.

The scriptural theme for this characteristic of masterful living is best described in Romans 12, where we read "Do not be conformed to this world, but be transformed...." It's even more obvious in the change that occurs between Romans 7 and Romans 8. In Romans 7, Paul is struggling to behave in a good way against the influence of his inner nature. In Romans 8 he experiences freedom that rejoices in the natural emphasis on the Spirit that comes from a nature that is based upon it. A shift occurs in a person's nature. The reference point changes and transformation happens.

In describing the transformation of character that comes from being full of Christ, it's appropriate to understand as best we can that new reference point. After all, being full of the Master means our lives will evidence the characteristics of God. The transformation to a new condition of Christ-likeness, then, becomes clearer.

Set Apart

GOD IS HOLY. BEFORE YOU START DESCRIBING CHARACTERIS-tics of what that means, just remember that simply put, God's holiness means that He is completely "other." Most of us imme-diately try to put more definitions on holiness even when we ascribe it to God. We may say that it means He is good, or pure, or loving, or just. All of those things are certainly true. But the bottom line is that God's holiness is best described as "other." Anything that is not of God, then is not holy. And the further you are from God, the less holy your condition.

God is His own point of reference. Pure love comes from God's holiness; pure goodness comes from God's holiness; pure justice comes from God's holiness. All these things are pure, complete, and whole because they come from God's nature that is separate from anything that would contaminate or dilute them. God is the starting point. Everything else is something less.

Proximity is important in appropriating God's nature in your life. When you choose to actively walk with God through a personal relationship with Christ, the Holy Spirit helps you to begin the *trans*-forming to become like God—holy, just like He is holy. Suddenly you begin to see how different God is from the dirty or compromised life that you've grown accustomed to.

God begins to bring you into a new condition that is like His condition of "other" or set apart. This happens because you are full of a Master whose chief characteristic is holiness. That becomes yours as well. Remember, though, it doesn't happen against your will. Being transformed in a new condition means you leave aside some characteristics of the old, and are made in a new condition because of your choice to live daily full of this Master. The effect is natural.

One of the difficulties of this kind of transformation is the possibility to become extreme in our own zeal. It's easy to fall prey to the temptation of thinking that because we are set apart we are different. To a degree, we really are different. But that can easily lead to disengagement and ultimately to antagonism, if we're not careful.

Here's how that works. If I am set apart, then I should use my own energy to be sure I do not associate with anything that I perceive to be impure or unholy. I work hard to stay separate, uncontaminated, and different from unholiness. I may even go so far as to establish rules to live by, requirements to live up to, and boundaries that I should not cross at the risk of being tainted by unholiness. As long as I stay dissociated with those things, I will stay holy and pure.

Very quickly you can see how that leads to a haughty attitude, and even to exclusivism. We are holy, therefore better. And we don't associate with unholy people or things. We become an exclusive clique.

What's worse is trying to impose that exclusivism on others—even other Christians—telling them that they are not as good because they do not avoid those same things. That's the worst form of legalism. It is completely inconsistent with the nature of God and out of synch with the transformation that the Holy Spirit is trying to accomplish.

Those lines of segregation are artificial boundaries that we have imposed on a work of God intended to bring healing to the life that is broken for lack of purpose. It creates segregation and divisiveness where God is trying to accomplish wholeness.

Yes, holiness means being set apart. But no, it does not mean becoming antagonistic in that separation. It is being transformed into a condition of otherness because the nature of the Master is finding effect, not because we are doing things that make us better.

Paul's description in the second chapter of his epistle to Colossians captures the order well. He clearly points out that we discard the old nature with its practices, and put on the new nature with its practices. The transformation of our nature precedes the altered behaviors. Actions will flow naturally out of a new condition.[1] We take off the coat of unrighteousness, with its resultant behaviors, and we put on the new coat of righteousness, with its behaviors. This is why we often associate holiness with pureness of heart.

Clearly there is a place for engaging in behaviors or practices as a means to affect our character. Repeated behaviors designed to affect our character are called disciplines. Over time, habits begin to have an effect on our nature. But Paul is trying to help us understand that the objective is a transformed nature. Out of that, new practices will come. Engaging in behaviors first is fine to the extent they are intended to find impact as a useful tool of God to transform our character. But it is a transformed character that is the priority.

The Holy River of God

EZEKIEL PAINTS A WONDERFUL PICTURE THAT CAPTURES THE spirit of this idea. In chapter 47 the preacher describes a river. The water is the otherness, or holiness, of God and God's people to the extent they reflect God's holy nature. The dirt along the sides is the security of what we have grown accustomed to in our own nature. To put it roughly, the water is the holiness of God, and the dirt banks are the world and our agendas. Each is clearly different from the other. They are different in their very essence.

Notice the source of the river. It's a river that starts in the temple of God. That's where God dwells. It has its source in God alone. It is not formed by human effort—committees, organizations, doctrines, or even a stubborn will. Holiness does not happen because you decide to do things that look holy. It doesn't come to be based on the force of your will to do more or to try harder. Neither does it come from the doctrine committees of churches or any other group. It comes simply and singularly from the heart of God.

Furthermore, no one has a corner on it. It belongs to no one and to everyone. Claiming a corner on the market of holiness presumes a favored position in what clearly flows solely and completely from God alone.

Now comes the invitation to step into the river. It is a magnetic draw. The man in the vision invited Ezekiel to come into the water. He agrees to—at least up to his ankles. He's definitely in the river—no question. But think about it: where are his feet planted? He's in the river but he's dependent upon the dirt under his feet. It's like a nice stroll along the water's edge. Not dangerous, and not too inconvenient. You enjoy the water, but you remain secure in your own foundation with your feet firmly rooted in the confidence of your own ability.

Have you ever stood ankle deep in the water of a fast-moving river, or at the beach of the ocean? You may enjoy the cool water but your feet are embedded in the sand. The water is rushing by, and in time, the sand begins to erode from under your feet. That's the water's way of trying to convince you to rely on it, not the dirt. When too much sand is washed from under your feet, your level of security is reduced. So what do you do? You change your footing.

We, in our vast insecurity and lack of trust, move our feet to find new and firmer soil on which to plant ourselves. The idea of not having solid dirt under our feet is frightening. Trusting in our own energy, abilities, and destiny is like that. And when we find it eroding, we move quickly to shore it up by re establishing our foundation on what we know, what we have grown accustomed to, what we can control, what is in our nature.

But it doesn't stop there. The man invites Ezekiel deeper into the river. So he responds and walks in knee deep. He's in the water, but still with feet firmly planted on what he knows—the dirt. And he watches the river flow by. But the water is stirring a bit more around his legs. Pushing a bit against him though not so much that he can't stand.

Again the invitation to come deeper into the holy flow of God. Now, waist deep. It's harder now. The water is roiling around him. Pushing him with greater pressure to give in to the flow of the river. That's the Spirit saying, "Trust me. Surrender. Be transformed."

Out of fear of being washed away, we remain firmly rooted with our feet in our own security. Oh, we're in the river. No doubt. We are believers, but we remain dependent upon our own ability to negotiate the many compartments of our lives in our Christian walk. So we stay in the river on our own terms. "I will be a Christ-follower but one who is in control!" Yet the spirit presses, pushes, prods, nudges, encourages to release. To surrender. To complete immersion.

And again, Ezekiel is invited still deeper into the river. And there he finds it to be a river he cannot cross. It's over the head. And in the middle of the river he cannot touch bottom.

Have you ever tried walking into the ocean or a river that is deep? There comes a point where you know it's over your head. You stand on your tip toes, desperately trying to keep control, to touch bottom, to keep from being carried along. Usually out of fear of drowning, or at least loss of control. Your feet scrabble for a toe hold. But there comes a point where you have to decide. And it's a big choice—to no longer trust the security of the dirt on the bottom, or your ability to reach it. Rather, to trust the river. To honestly believe it will hold you up. It is a crisis point. A massive shift of confidence from your own ability to that of the river. From your own control, to complete surrender. *I give up. I can no longer touch bottom. I can no longer control my stability.*

And in that moment, a transformation occurs wherein your own fear of loss gives way to exhilaration as you leave the bottom—now out of reach—and you really trust the water to hold you. And it does. Perhaps surprisingly. You knew it would, but now you are experiencing it. You are in over your head where your feet cannot touch the bottom. You are completely at the mercy of the water and you find it to be trustworthy. Suddenly you have a completely new point of reference. An entirely new sense of focus. Amazing. Yes, fulfilling. Freeing. And completely transforming!

In the middle of the holy river of God, where your feet can't touch the bottom, things change. Notice that the flow of the river is no longer a pressure against your side. There's no more splashing in attempts to get you to move with it. The water seems peaceful, because you are moving with it, not standing defiantly against it.

Notice also that you no longer fight, but you trust. You are motivated no longer by fear but by wonderment. You are part of the river. You are one with it, flowing at its pace and in its direction. You become a moving force with the holy river of God.

And most importantly, notice how your perspective changes. It used to be that as you remained with feet firmly planted in the dirt, you stood still watching the river flow by. Now you are in the river, watching the banks go by. Your whole reference point has changed.

In an act of your will to fully surrender, you have now become like the river. Immersed, saturated, completely in its flow. Now you watch the world go by with a different perspective. The banks on the side are no longer your security or your point of reference. They are now something you are passing by. And amazingly, wherever the river flows, new life springs up.

Our Part

SO WHERE ARE YOUR FEET? GOD'S INVITATION TO BE HOLY AS He is holy is an invitation to walk into the river—all the way, until your feet can no longer touch the bottom, until you are immersed. Way in, over your head—where there is oneness with the river. There you find buoyancy of the Spirit. There is perspective that is Kingdom perspective as you watch the world. You see things differently—not as things to be preserved or grasped, but as things that are transient yet in need of transformation.

Of course, it's easy to assume that this journey is one we work at, or that we may even engineer. That would be a false understanding. You see, the river is already whole. It is already differentiated from the desert around it. What we bring to the river neither enhances or substantially changes it. Nor are we a victim of the river. The only thing we bring to the holiness of God is our act of the will to surrender. We do not make the river what it is. We only surrender and enter it.

God will never overpower our will. But God will urge, woo, and nudge. And in response we have the ability to choose what condition will characterize our nature. We can stay on the banks. Or we can stay in the shallows. Or we can walk in full surrender to the overwhelming flow of God's transforming holiness, being immersed so that we reflect that nature.

A transformed nature is not simply a life well managed by controlling the activities you engage in. It is a complete immersion in the otherness of God's nature through an act of your will to surrender. The transformation is huge. From fear to wonderment; from fighting the river of God to flowing in harmony with it; from trusting in the security of your own nature to trusting in the nature of God to form and uphold you; from being rooted in the nature of the world as your reference point, to seeing the world with the eyes of God's nature which is now your primary view point.

And once our nature is transformed to reflect the otherness of God suddenly behaviors begin to follow. For we always behave out of who we are. Character always gives shape to activities. What we do is a reflection of who we are. So practices change and become symptomatic of a new condition, a new nature.

If we emphasize a transformed character as the sole characteristic of masterful living, the extremes of arrogance and legalism are an easy trap. This is not the whole story. It is only the beginning. A transformed character is the starting point but the river flows onward.

Scripture to Examine: *Romans 12:1, 2*

Theological Idea to Meditate On: *Otherness of God*

Danger to Avoid: *Sectarian legalism*

Questions to Ask Yourself:

1. Do a little inventory about your life. Are you in the river? How deep? What are the things you cling to that keep you from giving up control of your own destiny?

2. In what ways do you sense the Holy Spirit trying to urge you to deeper surrender to the flow of God's holiness in you?

3. What are the things that regularly try to lure you back to touching bottom and controlling your own formation and future?

A Prayer in Response: *"Oh Lord, I surrender to complete immersion in the river of Your holiness. Form my life in conformity to Your holy nature. Mold me as You will that my being shows evidence of Your handiwork. Separate me from the mundane that my nature becomes one with Your eternal purpose. Enter into my heart and fit me for Yourself."*

Chapter **Two**

RESPONSIBLE ENGAGEMENT

WE WERE EXHILARATED AS WE WATCHED THE PREPARA-
tions leading to the kickoff of a preseason game of
the Dallas Cowboys. Seated in the old Texas Stadium
awaiting the start of the game, we couldn't believe we were
actually at a game. This was the first time we'd ever been to an
NFL game.

It was early in our first year of full-time ministry in Dallas.
My wife and I were still discovering ministry with wide-eyed
idealism. We felt the thrill of being in a new city, a new church,
with many new experiences, and we never thought we would be
able to see the Cowboys in person. Of course, anyone who
knows the Cowboys knows that the fans are totally obsessed.
Now we were amid 50,000 of them! What an experience.

We sat in the middle of a particularly loud group. And the
loudest were right behind us—their knees in our backs and
their yells the loudest in the stadium, or so it seemed. They also
happened to be quite fond of their beer and nachos. After the
initial hype of the game start, a couple of them went off to get

more. It was hard to believe that a couple of these guys could actually fit in the seats.

At one point, one of the fattest, intently focused on the play unfolding on the field, jumped up to yell his disapproval of the player's run. Beer sloshed from the paper cup in his right hand, while the nachos in his left hand only stayed in the paper bowl because the gooey cheese glued them all together. The red-faced, beer-bellied man let loose a string of expletives that would have curled my mother's hair! I wondered, *Could he do any better than the athlete he was yelling at?*

Obviously I said nothing lest I incur his wrath. But I thought. I looked around some more and realized there were a lot more just like him. It was an amazing picture. Twenty-two well trained men on the field desperately in need of rest, and 50,000 specta-tors desperately in need of exercise. And many of them were shouting disapproval, advice, or orders.

Initiating a Relevant Way

THE PATH OF HOLINESS IS NOT A SPECTATOR ACTIVITY. IT requires engagement. Those who pursue masterful living do not sit in the stands growing unhealthy while chastising the errors or missteps of those who are fully engaged on the field of play. They get *on* the field. They get their hands dirty with engagement. Certainly they stumble and often fall short. But they are much more than spectators. They are actively involved. Responsible engagement balances the tendencies that can creep in when the goal of a transformed character is overemphasized. While the effect of equating holiness with character transfor-mation may result in isolation and separation from the culture, responsible engagement propels connection and participation in life around us. It proceeds from the scriptural pattern set by

God in the incarnation. "The Word became flesh and dwelled with us."

These two words—responsible engagement—are chosen carefully. By responsible I am not suggesting merely that the activity of engagement is "mature" or done responsibly. Of course, any engagement that a follower of Christ would engage in to influence his or her community would presumably be done in a mature and responsible way. But here I mean that we take responsibility for initiating the engagement.

It is often easier to act as if the grace and holiness that we enjoy is also available to someone else if they just come and take advantage of it. In this passive expectation, we sort of set a beautiful banquet in the banquet hall and wonder why people don't come to enjoy it. The thought of taking it to them in ways that are relevant to their need may never cross our minds. Yet for the one who is serious about masterful living, they cannot imagine not feeling the onus of responsibility for engaging with their community in whatever way necessary in order to make a difference.

The first and best example of responsible engagement resulted when we chose to do things our way and thus created separation from God. He didn't wait around hoping we'd come back. God took responsibility to initiate a plan to engage us again. God tried a lot of ways. He sent prophets, priests, kings, judges. Hebrews says "in many and various ways God spoke…."

Finally He chose a way that would be exceedingly relevant. He became one of us. Whatever it took, God assumed responsibility for engaging with us at any cost. His otherness did not leave Him isolated in transcendence. The incarnation was the manifestation of His imminence. God is other, and yet engaged. God is set apart, and yet initiates connection. God took responsibility to engage with our predicament. When He saw the estrangement created by our choice to sin, God's response was not to remain isolated in otherness, but rather to initiate engagement that would serve as a remedy to our condition.

Thankfully, God did not wait until we initiated some action to get closer to Him. If that were the case we probably would still be living in separation, far from God. Out of love God was compelled to assume the responsibility for healing the rift. He took action. He initiated, engaged, stepped out to bridge the gap and make it possible for us to be reconciled back to God.

The purpose of that initiative was completely centered on reconciliation. It was to bring back into closer proximity people who were once in union with God. Remember? At one time when we were created we walked in perfect fellowship with our Creator. The loss of that fellowship and union and the resulting estrangement burdened God with responsibility to act in making a way for restoring that fellowship of closeness.

His Priorities, Our Priorities

Masterful living, then, will not only set us apart, it will burden us with the responsibility to initiate relevant engagement. It is relevant in that it is shaped and guided by the unique conditions of people who find themselves far from God. Whatever fuels or causes the estrangement is the concern of people seeking to reflect the priority of the Master in reconciliation.

Generations ago, relevancy involved giving the poor the dignity of anyone created with the image of God imprinted upon them. It propelled Christ followers to run contrary to the prevailing tendency of becoming isolated in an enclave of separation merely awaiting the final extraction when Jesus came back for "His own."

Some of the most famous folks in recent church history took initiative to make a difference. As the Master became increasingly evident in their lives they were propelled to take responsibility for engaging the hurt, the broken, the disenfranchised in order to make a difference here and now, not simply to await the coming Kingdom.

Holiness is about proximity. It is not primarily about behavior. Masterful living alters us to become transformed in our character and it reorders our priorities so that what is important to God now becomes important to us. It puts us on the hunt for meaningful ways to narrow the chasm, reduce the separation, and reconcile people around us. God's priority is to reconcile people back into relationship with Himself. Because we live in proximity to God and our priorities are reordered that becomes important to us too.

This is not a forced priority. It is a natural outworking of a changed life. What breaks the heart of God now breaks our hearts. What makes God weep, makes us weep. We see with eyes formed in the image of Christ and when we see what He sees, we are compelled out of love to take initiative and engage in redemptive, creative, relevant ways that make a difference.

If the idea of a transformed character deals with the inner condition of your life, responsible engagement addresses the natural outworking of that condition in behavior and activities that are consistent with the priorities of God. It's for this reason that masterful people are often the first to respond to human circumstances in an attempt to meet a need. These people are servants of God. Their fealty is to God alone. Their nature is becoming like His and their priorities are being realigned with

His. So when God's crowning creation is hurting or broken, they are compelled to engage.

In recent history major issues have defined the activities of masterful people. Oppression of women was one major social hurt that stirred the heart of holy people. Discrimination of the poor, slavery and abuse. Economic injustice. Environmental carelessness. The sanctity of life. Lifestyle aberrations. Consumerism, hedonism, materialism. So many woes that percolate up in the hearts of human culture that is estranged from God. And when we see it our hearts break and we spring into action to address the disease.

Certainly these are public, social conditions that spurred masterful people into responsible engagement. But because personal character transformation is also of great importance, the pain of unconfessed sin and selfish living remains central to the burden we carry. Beyond the social ills is the personal brokenness and the need for engagement to bring grace and forgiveness to people.

You see, just as there may be an extreme pitfall for overemphasis on transformed character alone, there is also a danger in this descriptor. Singularly emphasizing responsible engagement will cause a skewed understanding of holiness as merely social activism. But what difference is there, then, between this and the civic club that does good deeds to help people out? Responsible engagement without a transformed character yields compassionate activities without the substance of a transformed life.

Living full of the Master yields a life that is not only sensitized to both, but gives evidence of these being woven into the fiber of living.

Scripture to Examine: *Luke 18:22*

Theological Idea to Meditate On: *Incarnation of God in Jesus*

Danger to Avoid: *Social Gospel/activism alone*

Questions to Ask Yourself:

1. Do you see hurt, brokenness, want, and deep need in people around you? When you see that, do you sense an inner urge to reach out in help, or do you wait to see if others take initiative?

2. Do you wait for someone to ask for help, or do you take initiative to bring wholeness and healing where you can? What does that require of you?

3. When you are actively engaged with others in bringing God's holiness, how do you know if this comes from an outpouring of the Holy Spirit from within your own heart, or is it simply a personal desire to act socially?

A Prayer in Response: *"Heal the condition of my own selfishness and make my eyes see what You see. Compel me as You were compelled, to bow in submission to every circumstance that the estranged would be reconciled; the broken would be bound up; the lost would be found. I hold loosely to the privilege of my own station, so that I may be ready to act unbidden when I see through your eyes."*

Chapter **Three**

HEALTHY RELATIONSHIPS

I SAT WITH THE MIDDLE-AGED MAN IN MY OFFICE AS HE quietly poured out his hurt. Occasionally pausing to swallow a welling up of sadness, he proceeded to tell me of his despair over his marriage, which had begun in a swirl of happiness and anticipation.

"We met in the most amazing way," he said. "It seemed we had so much in common that it was a sign from God that we should be together." He went on to describe how after a mere three or four months, she began to demean him, laying blame and accusations on him for a lack of joy and unity between them.

"It just comes out of nowhere when I least expect it! She tells me I have to give up all my friends. And what hurts most is when she attacks my character. She'll say, 'You're not loving.' 'You're not really committed.' 'You're a fake.'"

He was at his wits' end as he realized that having many things in common is not the same as deep unity in the most important relationship he could have.

Because Christianity is primarily relational, the Church

grows and is formed by relationships. First with God through a relationship with Jesus Christ, and then with one another in walking in the Way of Salvation together. And of course relationships with people who are not walking with Christ or part of the Church are always top priority albeit a challenge.

The essence of a relationship is determined by a sense of intimacy or oneness. Usually you don't hang out with people where you don't feel that closeness. It's the intangible element of unity that draws you to them. There's usually something at the deepest level that creates a bond—perhaps an experience, a goal, a way of thinking, or even a set of values.

Whatever it is, at the root of any relationship is the fundamental principle of unity. That's what drives you to know someone—to be one with them. Unity is what is broken when there is a schism between you and a friend. Unity is the fiber that weaves your life with that of another person. The greater the sense of unity, the closer the friendship.

That deep sense of oneness is not necessarily tied to particular likes or dislikes. In fact, often people who experience the greatest unity have very different preferences. But there is some elemental bonding that transcends the differences. You've heard the expression that "opposites attract." Certainly the principle behind that phrase underscores the fact that unity is more than things we have in common.

Healthy relationships are built upon oneness that allows for two or more people to be bound together. Trouble points in walking on the Way of Christ occur when relationships break down. Unhealthy relationships are the greatest cause of dysfunction and ill-health in the church. Perhaps it is two people feuding, or two groups at odds about the pastor's leadership, or criticism of one another that prevents unity from ever taking hold. Because Christianity is inherently relational, when unhealthy relationships prevail, unity is lost and the Christian faith is reduced to a set of beliefs and behaviors.

Unity within Diversity

MASTERFUL LIVING MEANS THAT WE ARE BEING FILLED WITH the Master such that we begin to understand the nature of unity. Healthy relationships are the natural outcome. This kind of unity is best epitomized in the image of the Trinity—God the Father, God the Son, and God the Holy Spirit. Three persons, yet one essence. Unity of being, but diversity of persons.

It is out of the diversity that unity can be forged. There is no unity apart from diversity. The very word "unity" implies that there must be sufficient diversity into which unity can be forged. So in reality it is only where there is a certain diversity that we may experience unity.

But this unity does not simply happen by chance. It requires a commitment and ongoing effort. And mostly, it requires mutuality: mutual submission and vulnerability. In the case of the Trinity, the Son submitted to the Father when He took the form of a human. The Father submits to the Son's work and intercession when He forgives and restores God's image in people. The Spirit submits to the Father in coming and being with us. You begin to see three diverse persons working in mutuality with one another. Yet they are essentially one—one in essence, though not in functions.

The unity that results in healthy relationships is formed around this principle of mutuality. Being mutually submitted to one another is the cornerstone. The Apostle Paul urges us to submit to one another—not in complete abdication of responsibility, but volitionally surrendering a claim on preferences for the sake of oneness. In honor, we prefer one another. In that act, we are acknowledging the essential nature of another person who is created in the image of God and essentially one with us.

I know it may sound confusing, but it is this diversity of function, role, personality, ability, gifting, and even circumstances that makes people who walk with Christ so amazing. Out of that diversity unity of essence can exist. But it can only exist when there is a gradual and ongoing dawning of the essential nature within us.

When the Master's image is being formed in ever deepening levels of identity the diversity of function becomes less important in light of the unity of being. In that condition, then, you are increasingly finding unity with others. The petty differences that cause dysfunction, broken relationships, jealousy, and strife fall away in favor of the oneness that rises between you.

Pursuing this unity is certainly counter to the prevailing emphasis in relational patterns of modern culture. We are told to find someone that has common interests. The typical excuse for breaches in relationships is "irreconcilable differences." Everything around you is telling you that unity is defined by activities that you and another have in common—likes, dislikes, priorities, vocations, hobbies, music. On and on.

If you are pursuing deep unity based upon superficial factors, it will elude you. Our culture has lost its depth and forgotten how to probe the deeper basis of unity. Masterful living presses us beyond what culture promotes.

The chief archetype of human unity is marriage. Is it any wonder that the Bible uses that image to establish the example of unity among people and even as the image of Christ's relationship to the Church? But notice that the fundamental principle of marriage is mutuality—be submitted to one another.

This is not to be reframed or misconstrued as meaning one thing for men and another for women. It means that both submit to each other. Complete mutuality.

The essence of healthy relationships, then, is unity. The primary principle in unity is mutuality. And the necessary act in mutuality is submission. All three of these steps are exemplified in perfect measure in God—the Father, the Son, the Holy Spirit. And when you live full of the Master, they are appropriated in you with the result that healthy relationships follow.

Of course, because relationships are dynamic and not static, you are always growing, changing, developing, deepening. And by nature that brings challenges, failures, and strains. We are never completely perfect in our ability to reflect healthy relationships because we are never able to reflect the Master with absolute perfection. But for each moment and every step, we may be completely or perfectly saturated with the Master to the extent we are capable until a new challenge or dimension urges us still farther on the path of masterful living.

That's what we are called to in perfect love. Not absolute perfection in performance, but complete saturation to the degree we understand.

Unity, Unanimity, and Uniformity

MOST DYSFUNCTIONAL RELATIONSHIPS EXIST BECAUSE OF some form of selfishness asserting itself on others. The counselors among us may help to clarify more deeply the nature of that selfishness. At its root, however, is the human will attempting to control or impose itself creating a breach between you and another person. Again, where there is a breach of oneness there is usually a broken relationship. Masterful living means a cure for selfishness.

I do not mean to suggest that unity means we all should think alike or look alike. Unity is deeper than behavior. It affects our behavior but it is not defined by it. Consider the difference between unity, unanimity, and uniformity. All are words that we tend to equate with oneness. Yet each is different.

Uniformity usually refers to behavior or appearance. We all wear the same uniform. We use the same words, we look alike, act alike, behave alike. It is the closest to "sameness." At its worst, uniformity turns into a conforming rigidity. Certainly there is a degree of uniformity that begins to creep into any close relationship. They say that after many years of marriage a husband and wife start to act alike, complete one another's sentences, or even look alike! In the organized church it's not uncommon for an unspoken expectation to be projected upon people to behave or dress or speak in certain acceptable ways. There's nothing wrong with our behavior rubbing off on each other as an expression of our bondedness. But when that becomes the definition of our oneness, and we begin to require that of another as the measure of unity, we've lost the intent of the Master.

Unanimity usually refers to values or ideas. We all agree as to what is important. We value the same ideas or priorities. We may not look alike, but we agree on the ideals. Usually unanimity is the result of give and take that allows for reflection and influence in accommodating differences and finding common ground. It requires a deeper level of relationship and trust between people.

Unity usually refers to the essential oneness that is innate within us and transcends the variety of different manifestations of ideas and behaviors. Even people who disagree on major concepts can still find unity. And certainly people who don't look alike or behave in the same way can find unity. This unity recognizes the basic oneness people share that transcends circumstances, place, and even values.

The ideal is that where there is uniformity there is also unanimity and unity. However that may not always be the case. Abuses of power, manipulation, dysfunctional relationships that are driven by selfish will and coercion may impose uniformity or unanimity where unity does not exist.

Conversely, while it might be tempting to say that the ideal would be for unity ultimately to manifest itself in healthy unanimity and uniformity that too is not always the case. The beauty of the mystery of God in us is the ability to find unity where uniformity and unanimity do not exist. It is in that diversity that unity is possible and most fulfilling. It transcends the differences of values and behavior. It places a priority on the person not the appearance or idea.

Mutual Submission

WHEN THE MASTER SATURATES YOUR LIFE, YOU BEGIN TO BE transformed in reflecting the same understanding of unity as is evidenced in His life. The mutuality of submission becomes the basis for unity among the diverse people with whom you form relationships. You may not like the same things, or speak the same way, but you walk in unity.

Differences of priority or behaviors need not undermine the fabric of the relationship and bring it to dysfunction. Masterful living allows your life to become a reflection of the unity exemplified in God that weaves diversity into oneness through the vulnerability of mutual submission.

This is not a formula for becoming a doormat. Living in a disposition of unity does not mean acceding to anyone's demands and losing your sense of self. Rather it is a willful choice to adopt a posture of submission by acknowledging the personhood of another. The resulting dignity and respect you offer them will transcend the difference you express over behavior or opinions.

When God created people, He did so by imprinting God's own image upon us. In a subsequent attempt to restore a relationship of unity with us, God approached us in submission. On the platform of mutuality. God respects our will, our dignity, our ability to choose voluntarily. And so in mutuality He humbles himself in submission to our will—offering unity.

Vulnerability versus Transparency

THE HITCH IN REFLECTING THIS KIND OF MUTUALITY IN A relationship is this: Unity requires mutuality; and mutuality requires vulnerability. When God in the spirit of mutuality pursued unity with people, He did so with great vulnerability. Vulnerability occurs when we open ourselves to another and show them so much of ourselves that they can even hurt us with what they see. God did that. God showed us His heart and passion—offering Himself even to the point of allowing us to reject and even hurt Him, which of course we did when we crucified Him.

Unfortunately, we have construed vulnerability as weak and unacceptable. So we replace it with transparency, wherein we may show people things about ourselves as a means to gain their trust and even manipulate their response. Transparency occurs when we show others something about ourselves—even something intimate—but never give them the ability to hurt us with what we show them.

Pastors have learned how to do this well. They may become

transparent to elicit responsiveness from people. They may show something of themselves as a means to make a point, to show their humanity, to garner support. That's not all bad in guiding people to truth. But when transparency replaces vulnerability in a relationship where unity requires mutual submission, we are on a sure path to unhealthy relationships.

Healthy relationships always begin to show when people embrace masterful living. It may not happen all at once. But gradually the ill health and dysfunction of interpersonal relationships at home, at work and at church will gradually give way to principles that reflect the Master who fills and transforms their life with a deep understanding of unity borne out of mutuality.

Scripture to Examine: *Ephesians 5:21*

Theological Idea to Meditate On: *The kingdom principle of mutuality*

Danger to Avoid: *Group relativism*

Questions to Ask Yourself:

1. In your behavior toward those closest to you, do you readily submit to their interests, or do you find yourself angling to get your own way, even by means of acting nice?

2. When you examine your inner attitude toward women, men, subordinates, or supervisors, do you find an attitude of true submission to them as a person? How do you recognize that?

3. Are there groups of people—women, other races, men, the aged—that you particularly struggle with to maintain an honest disposition of mutual submission? Why is that? How may you overcome that obstacle?

4. Who are people around you that readily come to mind who evidence mutuality? How does that manifest itself in a healthy relationship?

A Prayer in Response: *"Lord, take me past my obsession with superficial agreement. Let me find unity with others as I open myself to be known that I may know them. As You exposed Yourself in vulnerable surrender, may I find the joy of unity with those you love. Take me past the trifling of trivial tolerance and find the elemental health you created for us to embrace. In the name of the Three who are One."*

Chapter **Four**

WISE DECISIONS

T CAME OUT OF THE BLUE. A GOOD FRIEND WITH A DEEPLY troubled and burdened voice calling about her husband. "Anthony's gone. We don't know where he is."

"What do you mean 'gone'?" I said.

With more angst now, she said, "I mean, we've searched and called everywhere, but no one knows where he is. His car is gone and he hasn't called or been home for hours. The kids have both come and we're scared! And here's the worst. I checked and the gun box isn't here!" Her voice trembled.

"I'll be right over."

That call set in motion a long-term path of pain and trauma for a lot of people, but mostly for a dear family struggling to find wholeness and life. Late that night after long hours of prayer, tears, and unanswerable questions, the familiar sound of Anthony's car could be heard approaching. The kids rushed for the driveway, while the wife hung back—trembling with relief and anger, hope and grief. After the initial hugs from the kids,

Anthony admitted to spending the whole day up in the mountains with a loaded gun, wanting to commit suicide.

I looked Anthony in the eyes. "You've made a choice. The path ahead will not be easy, but I'm glad you chose wisely," I said.

On that day Anthony made a choice for life. I asked him, "What made you decide not to pull the trigger?" He said, "I kept hearing God tell me that He really does love me."

Everyday we all make life or death choices. Clearly they are not as obvious or immediately terminal as Anthony's. But each one has potentially as much impact. Wise decisions are made by people who are full of the Master. It's not that good decisions are simply evidenced by a successful or positive outcome. You see, choices that are wise are wise not just because of an expedient result. Wise decisions are decisions that in themselves allow for the vibrancy of life to flourish.

Ability to Choose

MOST IMPORTANTLY, SEEING WISE DECISIONS AS A CHARACteristic of masterful living implies that we possess the ability to choose. God has created us in His image. That image carries with it the ability for free will. We can decide. God will honor our decisions.

But as we have known from the beginning, every decision has consequences—good or bad. So, essentially the path of walking in holiness is up to us. Not that we form a holy character in ourselves; not that we appropriate salvation for ourselves; not that any source of grace comes from ourselves, but because we possess the capacity to choose we will make it possible for God to make us holy as He is holy.

Thankfully God is always at work pouring His grace on

us—whether we acknowledge that or not, whether we are Christians or not. His grace precedes our actions as He attempts to guide us. We call that prevenient grace, that is, grace that goes before, precedes, or influences us toward God's path. Through the prevenient work of God in nudging us, wooing us, encouraging us, whispering to us, clearly He is urging and helping our capacity to choose rightly. But ultimately that decision is ours.

For this reason, there is no real vibrant and whole relationship with God that is simply pre-established or predetermined. Journeying with God in wholeness does not happen without our active involvement in decisions. That's how much God respects the image of His own nature that has been imprinted upon us from creation. If God were to overpower our ability to make decisions in working out the path of our life would require that God undermine the very nature of His own image in us.

Decisions as a Partnership

ONCE WE ACCEPT THE REALITY THAT WE CAN MAKE DECIsions and have the freedom of will, then the question is how to make good decisions. Why is it that people who are full of the Master consistently make wise decisions? That's not to say that they are always expedient or right, but people embracing masterful living make good choices. Again, it's really about a relationship.

Many folks may assume that if they are sold out to God at some hyper level, then all they have to do is wait around for God to show up and arrange the circumstances for their good. I call that "blind passivity." In other words, you feel like you are so spiritual that certainly God will now work on your behalf so much that you don't really have to worry. Don't do anything, just wait. God will make the decision for you. God will work it out!

Alas, this is more abdication than wisdom. This practice of assuming that if you let go and wait for God to act is simply another form or determinism. As much as you may want to think of yourself as completely surrendered and open to "whatever God wants," it's really just another way of not accepting responsibility for a hard circumstance. It sets you up so you can blame God for a bad situation or so that you can redefine painful circumstances as merely something that God wanted to do to make you a better person. Either way, it takes you out of the equation and presumes God is a puppeteer. Blind passivity as an excuse for wise decisions is misguided.

Wise decisions are made in a responsible, healthy partnership with God. You see, when you are full of the Master, you are influenced by the nature, priorities, and heart of the Master in approaching decisions that need to be made. Whether it's a career choice, the choice of a life-long mate, course of study, relational matter, or any other decision that warrants careful contemplation, the Master who fills you will also influence you. The choice is yours, but the influence is evident.

Imagine yourself out looking at new cars. Your best friend is with you. As you admire a few models, you start thinking about which would be right for you. Your friend will not make the decision for you. It's yours to make. But having her there allows your decision to benefit from her insight, thought and wisdom. You would be foolish not to consult your best friend who knows you and your circumstances well.

Perhaps you are close to being bankrupt. Your friend advises, "You have no business looking at new cars. Don't do this." Again, it is your responsibility to make the decision; your friend will remain your friend no matter what you choose. She will give you advice and nudge you but never usurp your will.

You and your spouse have three children and a dog. But you love the two-seat sports car. Wisely you turn to your best friend and ask, "What do you think?" She says, "Not wise. Remember your family."

In the heat of your own passion, your partner helps keep you stable and with good perspective. It becomes a dynamic partnership of allowing your friend's wisdom to influence and saturate your decision. Of course your role is to listen and heed the wise counsel of your friend who loves you. You trust her, so you submit to her influence.

Now imagine that your friend is an all-wise God. You are walking in a dynamic, loving, submitted relationship with this One who's deepest desire is for your wholeness. You know that God loves you and you trust that His interest is for your good. So you are open to God's influence. As you approach a decision—large or small—the influence of God's nature and priorities affect your choices. So God's wisdom becomes active in your decision. This represents a mature responsibility in active recognition of partnership with God. And consistent wise decisions result.

Guiding Handholds

Two particular handholds become helpful in seeing daily decisions with masterful eyes.

1. Choose life.

What is a life or death choice? Not every choice is as obviously life or death as Anthony's. But every day we make life or death choices; every decision we make can perpetuate a mindset of one or the other.

Choosing life means we make decisions that allow for the grace and healing of God to work freely. In the most dramatic of moments, Anthony made a choice for life. He chose to allow God's love and grace to continue working in him to heal previous hurt, and to guide him in restoring wholeness.

When you choose life, you likewise remain open for God's grace to alter your heart, the heart of another, or to invade the circumstances such that wholeness and restoration can occur. Perhaps it's a confrontation and you are struggling with how to approach it. Grace will leave a crack in the door through which healing can find a way to wholeness.

When you choose life you also recognize the dignity of another person. Implicit in this choice is the recognition that God's image is within every person. Though their opinions may be extreme or even destructive, you still can see God's imprimatur upon them. Perhaps that image is clouded, warped, or dramatically covered by the effects of selfishness. But you look beneath that to see the remnant of God's image in them, and your choice acknowledges that as the source of dignity. So instead of treating another person with contempt, or speaking to them with a cutting or sarcastic attitude, you choose to recognize the image of God in them.

When you choose life, something within you flourishes. Your soul is fed. Your heart is strengthened. It doesn't matter whether your overtures for wholeness and restoration are accepted or not, within you the nature of the Master is released thereby transforming you a bit more.

Choosing death means you make decisions that close off the possibility of God's grace to bring healing. Had Anthony chosen to pull the trigger, he by his own self-centered choice would have closed off any hope of God's grace and love to bring healing.

Choosing death means that we usurp total control of the circumstances and presume to know all possibilities—and we determine there is no hope. It means that you do not believe there is any possibility of another person's heart being moved, changed, or influenced.

When you choose death, you close the door on any possibility of restoration or goodness. You sever the relational connection that people naturally have with one another because of the image of God in us all.

When you choose death, you undermine the dignity of another. You tear them down. You close them off and relegate them to unregenerate and hopeless chaff. In so doing you are denying the image of God within them.

Often it is not through overt denial that we choose death. Frequently choosing death takes the form of sarcasm, cynicism, or biting attitudes and words. Cynicism and sarcasm has no place in the life of a person committed to masterful living.

When you choose death—when you communicate through sarcasm or project a cynical attitude—not only do you cause harm to another person, but something within you dies. Life is drained. It ebbs away incrementally as the nature of a life-giving Master is repeatedly rejected in favor of isolation, independence and self-will.

2. STEWARDSHIP.

Because we have chosen to live under the dynamic influence of the Master, we by definition become stewards. Stewards are people who hold in trust and invest well on behalf of another. In this case we carry the DNA, the nature, the priorities of the Master. In an effort to be good stewards in this dynamic relationship of walking the journey, we are always asking ourselves the stewardship question, "How may I have maximum impact for the Master?"

Approaching decisions through those lenses will help to provide perspective that is not centered on our own selfishness. That is the nature of a good steward and in this case usually leads to wise decisions.

A steward makes decisions in a way that sees God first in all things. The idea of "first" has two dimensions.

First means prevenient. Prevenience refers to something that goes before. It is sequential in nature. For example, 1 precedes 2 and 2 precedes 3; 1 is prevenient to 2 and 2 is prevenient to 3. It refers to the sequential order or source.

A person living full of the Master has a stewardship mind in that he or she recognizes that the Master is the source of all—created all, ordered all, initiated all. That includes life, creation, and even the capacity to think and engage daily in the fullness of living. Because of prevenience, we then treat everything as a trust. We did not create it so we handle with care knowing that we do so on behalf of the one who is the source. All things that we possess—our personality, gifts, talents, environment, relationships, provision—we hold on behalf of the source of it all. We are stewards and that causes us to make decisions and use them all with a stewardship mind. To invest it, apply it, consume it as an effective trustee.

First also means pre-eminent. Pre-eminence refers to something that is more important, higher, greater. It is qualitative and hierarchical in nature.

A person living full of the Master has a stewardship mind in that he or she recognizes that the Master is above all—or as we often say in Christian circles, Lord of all. Whatever relationship, talent, gift, or circumstance we may encounter, a person living full of the Master approaches it with a stewardship mind because he or she knows that the Master is over it all; more important than anything; a higher priority than all of it.

Knowing this puts everything into perspective. It helps to ensure that nothing becomes all-consuming. Our balance is maintained when those things all fall into their proper place in light of the "over-allness" of the Master. We live, relate, and make decisions in a manner that is always subordinated to the Master.

In short, stewards make wise decisions when they see God as source of all we have and lord of all we do.

Wise decisions are not simply decisions that yield the greatest output. Rather, they are decisions made by masterful people who consistently choose life with a stewardship mindset. These are people in whom there is evidence of a maturing partnership between themselves and God in making decisions that are saturated with the wisdom that brings life.

Scripture to Examine: *Joshua 24:14-16*

Theological Idea to Meditate On: *Free will*

Danger to Avoid: *Rationalization*

Questions to Ask Yourself:

1. Do you accept responsibility for your choices, or do you find yourself always looking for someone or something to blame when things go wrong?

2. Do you struggle with sarcasm, hurtful remarks toward others, or dismissive attitudes which prevent you from seeing God at work in another person? What kind of people or circumstances foster

those in you? Can you hear Jesus's voice in sarcastic tones? How can you check yourself when that habitual pattern comes to you?

3. When confronted with a major decision, do you seek the wisdom and nudge of God within you first, or when all else fails? What patterns may best help you allow God to be a close partner with you no matter how small the choice that confronts you?

A Prayer in Response: *"Show me the consequences of my own choices, oh God, and give me the gentle nudge as You walk with me on the journey of living each day in partnership with You. Grant me deep awareness of Your wisdom as the basis of my actions, whether of small or great import. May my life and path be evidence of wisdom that is traceable to You whose counsel I seek moment by moment."*

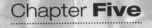

Chapter **Five**

INTEGRATED LIFE

MY WIFE CAME HOME NONPLUSSED. "I CAN'T BELIEVE what I heard today at work!"

She told me about a conversation she'd been part of with a teacher at the elementary school where she works involving another teacher, Cassandra. Since joining the staff, Cassandra had made it known that her Christianity was an important part of her life and that she and her family were vitally involved in church.

On this particular day, Cassandra had willfully disregarded state regulations for annual testing of the students in her class. She had prompted them with clues in an effort to improve their scores, as that would reflect better on her teaching. A fellow teacher, who was not a Christian but often heard Cassandra's claim to faith, witnessed the behavior and confronted her. Cassandra denied the claim outright.

Not only that. This same teacher had heard Cassandra calling her students inappropriate names and demeaning them in front of the class. The woman was frightened of repercussions and sought affirmation from my wife.

"I can't believe Cassandra not only would blatantly disregard the testing process, but actually treats the students that way. It's such a poor reflection on how a Christian should treat others," my wife lamented.

Probably the most often cited reason for people not wanting to go to church is because church members are hypocritical. They make big claims, but frequently don't live up to their own preaching. Of course, if you happen to be one of those members, you bristle. On the one hand you know that no one is perfect and it's unfair to be held to a standard that no one can ever realistically achieve. On the other hand, you know that it's true.

You along with everyone else in that church are not the standard of perfection that silences all criticism. Yet achieving perfection is not the reason for going to church anyway. After all, what better place for hypocrites to be than in church where they can grow and learn? Anyone who strives to grow and become more fully human, much less godly, will certainly earn the title of hypocrite at some point in their journey. Kudos to those who pursue it rather than merely wallow in the sarcasm of hopeless despair.

At the root of the criticism, though, is the recognition that the effects of Christianity have not completely found their way into the life of the people. Hypocrisy points to the condition of someone who is not complete. They behave differently than they speak. Or, more often, when they are in one situation, their behavior is different than when they are in another. In other words, they are compartmentalizing their life.

Most people see any incompatibility between various parts of life as the truest form of hypocrisy. And rightly so. Basically, though, it simply indicates that your priority and pledge to being filled with the Master has not yet permeated some part of your life. Holiness is the journey of Christ invading all parts of your life.

You've probably experienced another kind of compartmentalization. You see someone at church worshipping intently. Singing with all the gusto of a saint. Talking the spiritual language. At the altar praying intently. Even excited about the work of the Holy Spirit in someone else's life. Then they leave church and begin the work week, and it's like they're another person. Cutthroat, competitive, and even mean. They say it's because "business is business." But somehow the vibrancy of their life in the circle of Christians seems a bit hollow in light of how they live from day to day. You could even say they appear hypocritical.

Does this mean their faith is not alive? Does it mean they don't know the Master? Does it make them the hated hypocrite the world is referring to? No. What it does mean is that this person is on the way of understanding how to appropriate their relationship with the Master into the many dimensions of their life. Somewhere Christ has not been integrated into the totality of their being. They go to church and worship God but live like the devil. True hypocrisy starts where intent to grow ceases.

Clearly there is a category of people for whom the term hypocrite in the severest form is appropriate. Christ Himself called such people out and tagged them as being whitewashed tombs. These are folks who have honed the art of craftily misleading others into thinking they are something they truly are not. Unfortunately in the time of Christ this was leveled at religious leaders who should have known better.

Decompartmentalized

THE IDEA OF AN INTEGRATED LIFE EMANATES FROM THE completeness of God. God is whole, not segmented. And God is complete, not deficient. From this completeness, the words that the Master utters begin to make more sense: "...with all your heart, soul, mind, and strength." This does not refer to a formula that needs to be balanced with precision. Rather, it's a description of a completely integrated life that is saturated by a mature relationship with the Master.

The Master has influenced the heart, the emotions and spirit of a person, so that what is visible is obviously affected and different. Thinking and reason show similar evidence of a healthy partnership with God in permeating the disciplines of the mind. The body, as a creation and host of the presence of the Master, is also treated with appropriate respect and honor. And perhaps most importantly, the soul—the seat of the will—is formed by the mutuality and submission to the Master. Decisions, then, are shaped by the complete integration of the Spirit into the complete life of a person. The deficiency of isolation is being cured.

But integrated living is not just about Christ being woven into your life to cure deficiencies. It is also about dovetailing of one part of your life with another. Just as God is whole and not segmented, so also we in His image are being made to be complete, not segmented. Our reason and will begin to work in tandem with our body and spirit. The various parts of our being begin to affect each other and the wholeness in which we were first created becomes more and more real. Thinking and behavior are coherent; decisions are in line with emotions; emotions are not irrational, but reflective of deep and thoughtful convictions. To outsiders, your life is balanced, coherent, ordered, integrated.

All of this is based upon the reality that masterful living is not simply replicating behaviors that resemble holiness. It is not merely giving mental assent to propositions or regulations. And certainly it is not a grand balancing act of keeping the segments of our lives all properly fueled and measuring up to pre-determined standards. People who live like that divide their lives into compartments and wind up trying to live up to the rules of a faith that is a list of do's and don'ts. The frenetic effort to keep all the silos of life tended becomes exhausting. Mostly, it's a sure path to frustration.

More than To-Do Lists

CAN YOU IMAGINE A SERIES OF LISTS ON YOUR REFRIGER-ator—all outlining the steps to success in fulfilled holy living? Your job is to be sure that each day you comply with each item on every list. Doing so will ensure a meaningful, holy life. Well, that may be how it is at least in someone's warped opinion of fulfillment.

Anybody can live up to a to-do list. You could put a to-do list on your door for your spouse and say, "If you do all these things, then you will truly be my spouse!" Some random person might come along and fulfill every letter of the list. And they might do it with a high level of proficiency. But does that make them your spouse? I think not.

A relationship is not defined by compliance. Perhaps the sky-high divorce rate even among religious people is a result of reducing the idea of two people integrated with one another in marriage to a contract of do's and don'ts. A marriage is not made by compliance to behaviors any more than a holy person is made by living up to legalism.

Masterful living is inherently relational in nature; it's between you and your Master, as well as among the various parts of your self. After all, the truth you seek for fulfillment and wholeness in your life is not simply a proposition but rather a person. As you embrace the reality of that relationship; as you live in mutuality with that person; as you choose to allow your life to be saturated by the Master, then the various parts of your life will begin to blur together and cohere in purposeful completeness that is fulfilling.

The list on the refrigerator may be achieved, or not. In any case, it will probably look different than you expect and the wholeness of your life will come from the completeness your Master brings to your life as well as your own self becoming complete as you were created to be.

John Wesley got this right. A significant part of the genius of his movement was recognizing the holistic nature of our faith. It is the factor that most contributed to deeply transformed lives and perpetuated an ongoing movement which set his ministry apart from that of contemporaries like George Whitefield. Unless a person walked the path of an integrated life with the Master in a heartwarming experience, faith became cold and limp. Further, unless that faith permeated every dimension of a person's life—mind, emotion, and behavior—it would quickly become irrelevant and impotent.

On a visit to London a few years ago, our family visited Wesley's chapel and met with the Rev. Dr. Leslie Griffiths, Superintendent Minister. He was kind enough to open the museum the premises for us to explore and to guide us through. I was enthralled with the historic objects that brought deeper meaning to the world-changing impact of this minister. The kneeler, the pulpit, the riding chair.

At one particular point Rev. Griffiths stopped to show us what I thought was a rather mundane object. It was a simple bench used in the Foundry. I was not overwhelmed with interest until he showed me how it worked. Wesley had constructed special benches for his meetings. Each one had a hinge at the base of the back brace which allowed the back of the bench to pivot from front to back. Sort of a "reversing bench" idea. At first it appeared to be simply a novelty until the dean explained why these were built.

When people gathered for a church service, Wesley would preach the word from the front to all the people sitting in rows, as is our custom today. Most church buildings today are built around this model. In this fashion, Wesley opened the Scriptures and expounded the truth of God to the inquirers. He spoke to the cognitive dimension of their lives. Informing them. Telling them, challenging them, inviting them to think differently. He spoke to their minds.

The curator went on to tell us that at a certain point, Wesley would then ask the people to reposition themselves. Every other row would rise, pivot the back of their bench and sit facing the other direction. Now imagine a room where every other bench is facing backwards. The people are now knee to knee, eye to eye, engaging one another in pressing the cognitive truth deeper into the affect, the heart, the emotion of real life.

It is in social contact that the reality of the truth begins to form our lives and take root. It's out of this simple fact that Wesley was deeply convinced that there is no personal holiness without social holiness. Not merely a social holiness that engages the social issues of the day, but rather a social holiness that hammers itself out in the real relationships and interdependence of being part of one another's lives.

Now, face to face, the people are touching one another. Imagine a cognitive truth finding its way into the affective dimension of your life. Your emotions are engaged as you share with another person your real struggle in living out what you have just heard with your mind. In this social and relational construct the Master's image is being forged in you.

Then, as the people went away, Wesley called them to live out these newfound truths in behavior. Going into the marketplace with new thinking and new emotions will finally be secured in transformed behaviors. Fully engaged with the world in day to day work, a transformed life reflects the Master in action.

This made a lasting difference that is still influencing the world today. Touching the cognitive, the affective, and the behavioral made for a global movement that was unprecedented because people were transformed. When your life is full of the Master—your mind, your heart, and your action—you are becoming an integrated person.

Permeated by the Master

SOMETIMES WE USE MORE TECHNICAL TERMS TO DESCRIBE these dimensions. *Orthodoxy*, or right belief, touches the thinking of a life. *Orthopathy*, or right emotion, touches the affective part of a life. And *orthopraxy*, or right action, touches the behavioral dimension of a life. All three, woven into a person result in an integrated life that evidences the character and nature of the Master.

You may be a person who likes yogurt. Perhaps you've even tried it plain—no flavor, pure white, and no lumpy fruit.

Someone offers you some plain yogurt and it comes in a bowl. But you would like blueberry yogurt. So your kind server brings you a small cup of blueberries. You dump the blueberries into the plain yogurt. You even stir them around a bit so the blueberries are in all parts of the bowl of yogurt. Do you have blueberry yogurt? No. What you have is yogurt with blueberries in it. Look at it. It's white with a few blue spots where a berry is hiding. Take a spoonful and you will taste the plain yogurt and occasionally run across a round lump that bursts with flavor when you bite it.

But then you take your spoon and crush the blueberries, pressing them into the yogurt. The berries burst and deep purple juice permeates the whiteness of the yogurt. You stir and the juice and berries saturate the whole bowl. Even the color changes. It becomes blue as the berry juice and the yogurt are integrated. It is completely transformed. Now when you taste it, every bite has the flavor of blueberry. Some parts are stronger than others, but every part of the bowl has been influenced by the color and taste of the berries.

You see, it isn't until the life of the Master is pressed into yours, crushed in self-sacrifice, that you become an integrated person wholly influenced by the life of the Master and completely integrated so that the flavor permeates every part of your being. You are more than simply a person with a few characteristics of the Master sprinkled throughout. You no longer are a compartmentalized person holding strong pockets of flavor in segmented portions of your life. You are now transformed—a different color and flavor. Giving evidence of the Master who fills you. Filling you not to the exclusion of your own personality and characteristics, but filling you with a whole flavor that overcomes deficiencies. Changing your color with a wholeness that makes you completely masterful.

Scripture to Examine: *Mark 12:30*

Theological Idea to Meditate On: *The completeness of God*

Danger to Avoid: *Self-actualization as priority*

Questions to Ask Yourself:

1. Do you sense the presence of Christ with you as much at work as in church? Does your vocabulary, personal awareness, and behavior become different depending on who you are with? How may you allow the Holy Spirit greater access to the places, times, and circumstances in your life that you may ordinarily keep separate?

2. When you learn something new in your relationship with God, how do you find that it affects your life in other ways? Do you struggle to live out what you know to be God's desire for your life? How may the barriers between your thoughts, attitudes, and behaviors be taken down?

A Prayer in Response: *"Spirit of God, restore the wholeness in which I was first formed. Break down the walls that segment my life. Create completeness where I have caused separation. In embracing You, weave my life into the mosaic you once envisioned when You formed me in Your heart. Find every crevice and secret place to permeate with the healing fulfillment of Your oneness. Let no particle of my life be off limits to Your invasion. And may I be complete!"*

Chapter **Six**

PURPOSEFUL HEARTS

W E HAD TO MAKE A TRIP TO SCOTTSDALE FOR A BOARD
retreat. Flying was an option. But my wife and I realized
that by the time we went through the hassle of getting to
and from airports, renting a car, and all the stuff associated with
air travel, a six-hour drive from home might be a nice break.

Then I got to thinking that I could actually rent a car for less
than what it cost to drive the family car. So I made the reserva-
tion. "Give me an intermediate, modest car." I asked. A Ford
Taurus, just the ticket. Not too small and not too flashy.

I arrived at the rental location and was informed that they
did not have the car I requested. "We're sorry, but we took the
liberty of upgrading you." Fine, no problem, all good. I should
have been suspicious, though, when they told me my car was in
parking space no. 1. Normally my cars are in spaces 200 or above!

I walked to parking space no. 1, and saw there a brand new,
gleaming silver, mean-looking Nissan 350z. My mind whirled. I
was excited. Then I thought, *I should go back and tell them they
didn't need to give me such a fine car. I didn't pay for this. At*

least I should pay the difference. All noble and pure. That thought lasted a nanosecond. Not even enough time for me to break stride on my way to the high-powered sports car.

I drove home to pick up my wife. She wasn't so impressed but patiently accepted my enthusiasm. We headed out across the desert to Arizona. What a car! I kept telling her, "I love this car!" The handling was superb. The power was incredible. "I love this car!" The sound system was amazing. Gas mileage was really good. And it could go really, really fast! What a car to have on the long straight highway across the Mojave. For the few days we were there I often repeated how much I loved that car. It performed exquisitely. I was so impressed.

When we got back to California, we took the Nissan 350z back to the rental location (me thanking the rental company abundantly). I climbed into *my* car, started it up, and headed out. Now, my daily driver at the time was a forty-year-old Cougar. Its ball joints squeaked; the top leaked; gas mileage was horrible; handling was very poor and I dared not go too fast. Yet I caught myself sighing in deep satisfaction, "I love my car."

At the risk of trivializing a relational and deep life principle, I was surprised by the lesson. You see, I loved the 350z—but I loved it for its performance. What would happen when it broke down? What would happen when it couldn't perform as new? What would happen when another model came out and made this one obsolete? What would happen when my standards grew accustomed to it? What would happen when the novelty wore off?

I had poured my sweat, time and sometimes blood into my old Cougar. I knew it inside and out and had touched most of the parts on it. It was a classic. I had spent time with it. It wasn't just "the car," it was "MY car." My love for the car transcended its

performance. There was part of me in it. I accepted its inade-
quacies and loved it for deeper reasons.

Love Is a Motive, Not a Response

GOD LOVES YOU. NOT BECAUSE OF YOUR PERFORMANCE, BUT
because His image is in you. When you limit God's love for you
to how well you perform, you cheapen His love and hold yourself hostage to your own ability to do well. It's quite arrogant
actually. In effect you limit God's love for you only to the level
of what you can do. In this fashion you actually redefine God
and force Him to live under your constraints.

Yet God's love is not tied to performance. It is not determined by how much you contribute in time, money, or exper-
tise to anything—especially His enterprise on earth. God's love
is not a response. It is a motive.

God created us out of love. His love was purposeful and it
compelled Him to act. It was the depth of that love that motivated our existence to begin with. And that same love was the
motive God had in giving us freedom to choose.

Upon choosing selfishly and creating distance between
humans and God, we caused Him deep hurt , sorrow, and
mourning. Our action was a rejection of the very purposeful,
creative love of God. The passion of Christ is a glimpse into the
depth of God's purposeful love and the effect of our rejection.
Yet our rejection did not stop God's flow of love. Because it is a
motive giving purpose to His action, God continues to love no
matter our response. It is not tied to our performance, thankfully, because we have not really done well.

Out of love, God was motivated to create a path for us back
into proximity with Him. That is the path of restoration in which
we are reconciled back into a right relationship with the One

whose love first created us and imprinted us with His image. Out of love, God restores the wholeness and cures the illness of sin and selfishness. That is His purpose in all His acts toward creation. Out of love, God completes the deficiencies in our humanness caused by the sin of estrangement from Him.

Love is a motive, not a response. It is not reacting to the great performance of a person with the contingent phrase, *I love you*. "You do so much for me—I love you." "You make my job so easy—I love you." "You always have a nice thing to say to me—I love you."

Caused by God, love is the initiating motive for behavior and action that sees the hope and possibility of completeness, restoration, wholeness, and proximity with the Master. Living a masterful life is evidenced by behaviors and actions that have a purpose, and that purpose is very simply love. Not contingent love. Not in response to performance. Not even determined by the severity of a need. Simply love that is a motive and gives purpose to your engagement—with others, your job, your family, and even yourself.

This purposeful heart of love is not something that is acted out. It's not a skill that is acquired. Rather it is a condition of the heart that is saturated with the Master whose love permeates a masterful life. It is the core of your being. It is the culture of your heart. It is the economy of your life.

Love Is the Purpose

I ONCE HEARD A PROFESSOR DESCRIBE IT THIS WAY. LOVE IS the house in which we live and faith is the porch that gives access to the house. By faith we allow the Master's nature and DNA to absorb us and welcome us back into the house which is our home. This was the condition in which we were created. And it is the condition for which we were purposed.

Faith that the Master can actually reform the condition and culture of your heart is not casual. It requires a willful surrender of selfish motives at the deepest level. Often that is characterized by a downward path of surrender and brokenness wherein self will yields to God's. But upon entering the house of love your heart is daily being reformed and more deeply acculturated to the first purpose for which God lovingly created you. You are learning and adopting the values of the home in which you live.

The effect of this reconditioning is that love now compels your actions. It is becoming the purpose for which you live. Not to achieve, but to love. Not to acquire, but to love. Not to direct, but to love. Certainly the pragmatic application of a purposeful heart will result in many things that are accomplished and even resemble achievements, directing, or accomplishments. But when examined and experienced by others, the core motivation is clearly love. Selfless, all consuming, motivating love. Just like the Master.

People on the way of holiness reveal purposeful hearts. Everything they do is tied to one core, motivating purpose. The nature that characterizes what they do is symptomatic of one deeply motivating purpose. The effect in their environment or among the people around them is similarly imprinted with their purposeful condition. They are full of the Master whose purpose is love. They too operate with purposeful hearts, having been affected and transformed to reflect the self-giving, sacrificial love of their Master.

Yet it was that same love that resulted in the Master being rejected and spurned. It was so offensive to an ego culture and selfish human condition that it became intolerable. Of course the same fate may also await those whose hearts are similarly purposeful. Rejection for no apparent reason. Illogical offense. Discriminating isolation. Why? Not because of the quality or value of the purpose, but because a purposeful heart motivated by love is an offense to the selfishness in which many choose to live. It strikes at the heart of an estranged life that is not full of the Master and which does not accept the idea of motivating love. A purposeful heart of motivating love disrupts the economic balance of a life or culture that is built upon contingent love, self absorbed love, love that is merely a response.

In that dynamic clash the pain, mourning, suffering and even passion of your purposeful heart will be tried and at times broken. But because it is a motive not a response, you are more deeply formed in the image of God and walk on in masterful living.

Scripture to Examine: *1 John 4:7-8*

Theological Idea to Meditate On: *The love of God*

Danger to Avoid: *"All you need is love."*

Questions to Ask Yourself:

1. Think about the people you love. When you examine the reasons why, what do you discover? Is it because of what they have done for you? Is it because of what you can gain from them?

2. Do you find that your love for others compels you to ask how you might engage them? Do you see them as people carrying their own burdens or as commodities for your gain?

3. What would need to happen within you so that your disposition is formed more into conformity with God's in being motivated by a deep love for others?

A Prayer in Response: *"Jesus, Your love drove You to Your destiny. Though for unworthy souls like mine, Your nature could do no less. Create* *in me a heart that loves; not for what it may gain in return, but for what has been forged from within. Compel me by love that does not expect but only gives. Secure me in love that acts, not simply reacts. Show me through my circumstances the love that motivates and gives for no apparent cause. This is the love that will form me. This is the love that will secure me. This is the love that You give me."*

Chapter Seven

SERVANT LEADERSHIP

THE YOUNG LADY CAME INTO THE CLASSROOM, ORGA-
nized her notebook, recorder, and coat at the table, and
then sat down with an expectant look. She was ready to
take notes, ready to learn. I could tell by her demeanor she was
serious about her graduate program and was a real go-getter.

At the beginning of every class, I like to introduce myself to
each student. I made my way over to her to shake her hand and
find out a little bit about her. We were going to be spending a lot
of time as a group in this class over the next nine weeks. I like to
know the people who are walking the journey of learning and
development with me.

I approached her, "You look totally ready for class. Is this
your first in the MA program?"

"No, but I've talked to others and I am so excited about
taking this class!"

"Really. And why's that?" I responded, immediately encouraged that someone was so excited about being here.

"Well," she said. "I want to learn about servant leadership. I've heard it really works."

The truth. She was here because she was interested in mastering something that she had heard would make her better, more efficient in her position. To her, servant leadership was something that worked; something that would increase the bottom line; something that would get her noticed. I knew I had my hands full.

I didn't know her circumstance or her dreams. But I did know that she was approaching the whole concept of servant leadership as many people do today. They assume that it is simply a style of leadership; a set of skills to be mastered in order to maximize their influence on the job and increase the bottom line.

For these folks, servant leadership is one of many models of leadership. You sort of go shopping for a style of leadership that will best suit your personality or your situation. For them, the key to good leadership is finding the right "model" to use in order to be successful. Servant leadership takes its place alongside other styles like collaborative leadership, or situational leadership or directive leadership or autocratic leadership.

In reality, servant leadership is not a style at all, but a condition of the life of one who is influencing others. *Servant leadership is influence that reflects the inner condition of a servant in empowering and up-building others to fulfillment.*

Servant leadership deals with the condition of your identity, not simply the performance of leadership activities.[2] This pattern of inner condition giving rise to external actions is one that is prevalent throughout the Scriptures. The most overt example is found in the very person of Christ—the mind of Christ, to be exact. Philippians 2:5-11 is the best place to see the call to a condition, a disposition, an attitude, a mind as the basis and motivating platform for substantive behaviors that result in transformation.

Apart from the other characteristics in the wholeness of masterful living, this characteristic could easily wind up as simply a style of leadership that can be mimicked at high levels of proficiency by smart people applying their skills to the work situation. This characteristic, like all the others then, must be seen in balance with all the others as a descriptor of a person who is masterful.

Servant versus Slave

OFTEN PEOPLE PUT THE TERM SERVANT IN A SIMILAR CATegory as slave. Clearly there is a difference but usually in popular conversation both describe the function of someone who does menial labor for another person. This is particularly true in some cultures outside North America.

A few years ago while speaking to a national conference of business leaders in Latin America, I asked the three hundred business persons to give me quick, off the cuff words to describe their image of a servant. Here's what they came up with.

- Laborer
- Gofer
- Obedient
- Subordinate
- Invisible
- Service
- Meek
- Uneducated

These were all words that came to their minds. And they were not unique. Even in the twenty-first century North American or Asian or European culture, often words like these come up. We have been programmed by a hierarchical mentality to apply administrative power to various words like this one. And of course, that power is always more concentrated at the top levels and less concentrated at low levels of an administrative structure. So because human predisposition is to put the term servant at the bottom of the organizational chard, the concept of servant is void of power, influence, and status.

In establishing the fundamental nature of a servant, the difference between servant and slave is huge. Understanding it in the context of a broader definition of leadership is also quite important. Leadership is simply influence. Much like salt influences its surroundings, so also leadership influences it environment. It has an effect. The fact that there is an effect is leadership. The method as to how the effect is achieved is usually the subject of most leadership discussions and that leads to styles and performance.

But since servant leadership is influence that reflects the inner condition of a servant, we now are focused on that condition, not merely the outcomes. Servant leadership starts with the condition of a person, not the skill or activities.

Slaves have a subordinated relationship with their master due to coercion. They have no choice or recourse. Slaves are owned and forced into submission by threat, pain, or simply for lack of any other options.

Millennia ago, a kind master would sometimes set the slave free. On occasion when that happened, the slave might actually come back to the master and voluntarily pledge fealty to the master bonding themselves to the master. They were no longer a slave, but now a bond-servant.[3] This was quite a different condition. Still the bond-servant would occupy the same space, do the same things, and behave in the same manner toward the master. However, now they did it voluntarily not out of coercion.

The difference between a slave and a servant, then, is simply a matter of the will. A servant is voluntarily subordinated to a master to whom they pledge fealty. Behaviors may not change. But the inner condition does. And when a person voluntarily pledges to be the servant of another, the condition of the servant is altered. In this way servant leadership may use a variety of styles of leadership. But it is the condition of the person being reflected in those leadership behaviors that makes them a servant leader.

You may be an autocratic leader, or a collaborative leader, or a directing leader, or a theory X leader—and still be a servant leader. The real issue is not the style but the inner condition of your life and how that condition is reflected in whatever style of leadership you apply. You may ask, "How is the condition of a person affected by being a servant?"

Servant/Master Construct

WHERE THERE IS A SERVANT, THERE MUST ALWAYS BE A master. If there is no master, there can be no servant. The word itself loses any meaning apart from that. This servant/master construct has a deep impact on a person who commits to being a servant. Masterful people have pledged to be a servant of God. Immediately the servant/master construct is set up and the effect begins to be seen both in the person and in the influence they exert.

Being a servant is not simply doing the things that the

master wants. Slaves and mercenaries can do that. What makes servants unique is that they have voluntarily submitted themselves to a master. It is much more than negotiating a deal to perform certain services for another person. Servants have emptied themselves of their rights and humbled their wills to that of another.

In emptying rights, they have voluntarily and willfully chosen to release their grip on the rights that naturally accrue to their position, age, education, or status.[4] In humbling their will, they have voluntarily bowed their agenda, ambition, and personal desire to that of a different will. You cannot grip your personal rights and still serve another. And you certainly cannot assert your own will and still fulfill that of another.

I have run across many people—as you may have—who claim to be a servant of God. Yet they behave like they are protecting themselves from the imposition of others. Why do so many Christians sue one another? They are grasping their rights. Why do so many church leaders negotiate tenaciously for a larger salary? Some of them feel it is their right. Why are there so many fights—even in Christian organizations? Because someone feels their rights are being violated and think they must defend their rights or no one else will. Yet when we swear fealty to God, do we not give up our rights? Do we not open our hand in release and relinquish claim on what we gripped so tightly? Are we not called to empty ourselves of our rights in putting on the servant mind of Christ?

I'm not talking about being a door mat. But I am saying that when we say we are a servant of God, it means something. It means our disposition is not "clingy." We do not grasp at anything holding tightly to it as if somehow it is our salvation—position, status, salary, possessions. The world may say it is our right.

But when we voluntarily empty ourselves we do not hold onto our rights any more than Jesus held onto His equality with God.

And you have probably seen many people whose greatest struggle is to get their way. Sometimes we call it stubbornness. That can be a good trait unless it becomes obstinacy, self will, or disobedience. Voluntarily humbling your will to that of another—even God's—is a painful, hard thing. It is counter to our human nature which wants to assert itself at every turn. To bow rather than assert is the path of brokenness that a servant must walk. That is what took Jesus off into isolation so frequently. That is what the great struggle was all about in the garden before He died. A battle of the wills. It is not easy. But the nature of a servant is forged in the battle of the wills. Two wills cannot coexist.

The Effect

TWO THINGS HAPPEN WHEN YOU BECOME A SERVANT. FIRST, your nature is transformed into the likeness of your master. This is a natural consequence. The master's nature begins to rub off on you. In pledging fealty to a master, either intentionally or unintentionally, you expose yourself to the nature of that master. You become susceptible to influence. You begin to become like your master. That's because we tend to become like the ones that are most important to us. When someone or something is important to you, then you will take on their characteristics. The nature of that master will find its way into the core of your being and your nature will become similar. It's not so much something that you do as it is just the natural effect.

Second, your priorities will become aligned with the priorities of your master. What's important to your master will become important to you. Again, it's a natural effect of serving a master. It's not that you work hard to realign your activities and priorities but it just happens. Here's what this all looks like.

When you voluntarily submit yourself to your master, your nature immediately begins to be influenced by that master. There is a nature or character associated with a person or thing. That nature or character begins to rub off on you because you have opened yourself to its influence. After a time, you will begin to reflect the nature of your master. If that does not happen, you have not submitted yourself. A servant is submitted. A servant is emptied and humbled to the influence of the master. The effect is natural.

Likewise, your priorities will begin to be realigned. Your master's mission will become yours. That's part of why you choose to serve that master. As you approach the day to day activities, you will begin to see them through the eyes of your master and try to figure out how to best use them for the good of your master's priority.

So now you come to the most important question you have to ask yourself. It's simple.

"Who's your master?"

Think about it. Imagine the possible masters people may choose to serve. In many cases the masters people serve become so by default rather than intentional choice. Here are some of the most common masters people may serve.

- Money
- Self
- Position
- Power
- Others
- God

Each of these possible masters has a nature attached to them. And each has a set of priorities. If you serve one of them, you will begin to take on the characteristics of their nature and you will begin to operate according to their priorities. That's not a threat or prediction. It's just the natural effect.

Show me someone who serves money and I'll show you someone who is greedy and strives to accumulate.

Show me someone who serves self and I'll show you someone who is egotistical and behaves arrogantly.

Show me someone who serves position and I'll show you someone who is manipulative and climbs as high as possible.

Show me someone who serves power and I'll show you someone who is abusive and always has conditions attached.

Show me someone who serves others and I'll show you an insecure person who seeks always to please others.

Show me someone who serves God and I'll show you someone who is Christ-like and seeks to reconciliation.

I am not suggesting that these are all mutually exclusive. That is to say, it's not a case where you only have one influence in your life. Really, we all deal with all of these. Each of them wants to be the master. Some have louder voices than others in luring you or wooing you. I can tell you that God's voice is a small voice. Others are considerably more obnoxious.

The issue is not whether you have to deal with them all. You will. The question is which will be preeminent in your life? Which will most influence you? Which will order your priorities and shape your nature? Which will be the master?

Depending on which you choose, the others will fall into subordination. You'll still have to deal with God if you serve money. You may use God or religious things to get you good connections and deals to make more money. But God will have to be dealt with. You'll still have to deal with money if God is your master. But you will deal with it in a manner that is subordinated to your master and His nature and priorities. You may use money to declare your priority. That's called tithing. You may use money with a nature that reflects Christ in generosity and with great stewardship. Whichever you choose, the others will fall into place in light of the Master. You will use them with a nature that reflects the nature or character of your master. And you will use them consistent with the priorities of your master. So choose well whom or what you will serve.

You see, God's nature is holy. God's character is most fully expressed in the person of Christ. We see God visibly in Christ. In Christ we see God's holiness. In Him we "behold" the glory of the Father.[5] In becoming human, Christ let go of His rights as God and humbled His will to God's. It was cemented in the garden before His death, when He said, "Not my will but yours be done!"[6] His nature was the full reflection of God's nature. And His priorities were ordered by the Father. That's why He came to begin with. God's number one priority was to restore people back into a relationship with Him. So in serving the Father, Christ's priority also became to restore people at any cost; whatever it took.

We often confuse the deeper meaning of the word servant. Sometimes we say Christ came to serve, and He did. He ministered to the needs of people chief of which was the need to be reconciled to God. But in serving people, He was performing acts of service or ministry. He was not their servant. One is a function of activities, the other of identity. Likewise our popular language is full of references where we serve one another, we provide service to others, we even ask, "How may I serve you?" But all of that is in reference to activities that we may be able to perform to assist. It is not a reference to the basic identity of a person.

If you willfully choose to be a servant of God, it will be a similarly dynamic journey of day to day living—opening yourself to the nature of God and increasingly reflecting Christ. And your priorities will begin to become realigned so that what you used to think was important will become less so. And suddenly you'll find yourself thinking about things that are important to God. Like people who are lost, broken, hurting, needy. You'll begin to carry a Christ-like nature into whatever you do, no matter how menial. Your daily activities will begin to reflect Jesus because you are susceptible to the influence of your Master's nature and priorities.

When people look at you, they will certainly see behaviors that are being reformed and focused on new priorities and they will admire them. But mostly they will begin to be curious about the personality of the Master whose nature is becoming evident in the artwork of your life. The Master is in you. Your nature and priorities are increasingly reflecting Him. That's masterful living!

Scripture to Examine: *Philippians 2:5-11*

Theological Idea to Meditate On: *The servant mind of Christ*

Danger to Avoid: *Style of leadership only*

Questions to Ask Yourself:

1. When you take inventory of your life's actions, to what "master" do they seem to point? Do you embrace as you primary reference point what your behavior indicates is your master? Who's your master? What are the characteristics you expect will become evident in you because of your master?

2. If you have intentionally declared that your master is God, do you find yourself still gripping control of your future and personal

agenda? How might you more readily learn the willful act of surrender?

3. In what ways are the priorities of your life consistent with what you say is your reference point—your master? When you ask others what they perceive your master to be based on your behavior, what would they say? Will you voluntarily surrender to the inner nudge and will of God in the decisions you make today? Tomorrow?

A Prayer in Response: *"Lord, make me like You. You are a servant, Lord, make me one too. You are my Master, so form me to reflect You. I pledge my fealty to You alone. I release my rights, I surrender my will. Let my life move at Your impulse and may my priorities be ordered by Your desires. I will serve You and none other. I will serve You that I may reach to others, for that is Your will. Let me bow as You bowed, and pray as You prayed, 'not mine but Your will be done.'"*

Chapter **Eight**

MEANINGFUL WORK

TEN BILLION! $10,000,000,000! IT'S MIND-BOGGLING. That's what Bill Gates contributed to vaccines to reduce childhood mortality rates. Oprah Winfrey has donated $12,000,000 to help Morehouse College develop black men for leadership and service. Warren Buffet has given away $37,000,000,000 to five charitable foundations.

Wow! By any measure those are amazing feats. Valuable contributions to society and to the needs of people. If anyone can claim that what they do has value, Gates, Winfrey, and Buffet can. And they represent a small fraction of the people who daily donate, give, tithe, contribute or otherwise selflessly divest themselves of wealth for a good and worthy cause.

Think about it. With the massive contributions of just these three people, someone could write a book just about the lives that are being impacted. That amount of money can make a significant dent in the causes they are committed to.

At first glance there are two reference points that most of us use to determine that these acts of generosity have value. First is the amount of money. The amount of these contributions is mega-huge, and the value it brings is mega-huge. Goodness, can you imagine what even one million could do? Most of us can't, much less multiple billions. No question that sometime in the next ten years vaccines will be developed that will save the lives of countless children. There is no doubt that hundreds and thousands of young black men will grow, develop, and rise to leadership because of the money given. The outcomes are immeasurable.

Second is the cause for which the contributions were made. No one could ever hesitate at the idea that $37 billion to charitable foundations can multiply in effect around the world. All of these causes are noble, altruistic, and wonderfully high in moral quality. The fact that these are such good purposes makes what these people do highly valuable.

Either of these reasons—the amount of generosity or the cause they give to—is enough to make the donors feel that what they have done is truly meaningful. Clearly these are high profile cases that few others can match. However, everyday people do equally noble and morally good things. In most cases the people who do them feel that what they are doing is valuable. And they find meaning in their actions either because of the amount of what they do or the cause to which they give themselves.

You may be somewhat like this. Not at this level, but you use similar measures to determine the value of what you do. You may look at "how much" or at the "cause" and in so doing you evaluate the value of what you do by the outcome it has. Perhaps you even evaluate whether your job is meaningful based on the outcome it has or the amount you give of yourself to it.

Our contemporary culture applies an outcome-based grid

to the process of assigning value. If what you do is big and has a noble cause then perhaps you feel it is meaningful. And certainly if the outcome is good and it produces great results, you walk away feeling fulfilled and valuable.

Outcomes, amount, or cause are usually the basis on which we determine the value and meaning of what we do. Clearly it is normal to assess an outcome valuation to doing. After all "doing" by nature calls to mind some type of result. But the one variable that is left out—and it is perhaps the most important—is the why the motivation that initiates.

What happens to the many for whom a large amount of anything, money, time, or product are impossible to provide? What happens to the many for whom a noble cause beyond simply making ends meet is only a pipe-dream? Or what happens to the many who are not noticed, who don't stand out from the crowd, who are average at best and cannot convince whoever is judging that they are a valuable member of the team? Are those people relegated to work that is not meaningful? Do they have value? Will they have engagement in meaningful work?

Meaning More than the Bottom Line

MOSES WAS SUCH A MAN. HE HAD EVERY CHANCE. HE WAS raised in a palace as a king's grandson. He probably had anything he needed and all he wanted. He was privileged and had a bright future as a member of the royal family. Yet no amount of privilege or possession provided him with meaning. He tried to find meaning in a cause, the cause of his people. But it failed him. Lack of meaning resulted in him wandering for years as a common shepherd in the desert. This was menial work. Mundane at best. Unnoticed and worthless at worst. Yet it was out of this context that Moses was formed when he encountered God at the burning bush. In the contrast between affluent privilege and isolated routine he came face to face with the source of true meaning. It was not in the outcome but in the One who called him.

Moses considered his work from that point onward as being meaningful. Not because he knew the outcome. Not because delivering people from slavery was a compelling possibility, and certainly not because it was a coveted position—he had argued *not* to do it. It was meaningful because of the fact that God had called him to it, regardless of the outcome.

You see, what you do is meaningful not because you may add to the corporate bottom line, or the organizational key performance indicators, or even the quantity of product. For those who are Masterful, work is meaningful because of the call to do it. It is the call of the Master that gives what you do value and meaning. The very fact of God calling makes it enough to be meaningful, no matter the outcome.

In a culture defined by outcomes, bottom lines, and objective product, this is a very difficult principle to embrace, much less to live by. When your output is average or unremarkable, you may still find value in what you do because God has called you to it. That in itself makes it meaningful. For masterful people, meaningful work is based upon the call of God.

Responding to the Caller

LET'S TAKE A CLOSER LOOK AT THIS. THE IDEA OF CALL IS very similar to the concept of vocation. Often we equate the idea of vocation to the function of a job. Someone asks, "What's your vocation?" You answer with the title of the job or the category of job you happen to hold. Vocation is determined by position and function.

Yet the idea of vocation or call has a much deeper meaning. Long ago the term vocation was reserved only for those who were headed into the pastoral office or the priesthood. It was a contemplative path to church leadership. The influence of this understanding can still be seen in the Roman Catholic Church today. When speaking of the future of the priesthood, you may often hear church leaders say that "vocations are down." In other words, the number of individuals who give testimony to a call to the priesthood is down.

With the Reformation came the idea of the "priesthood of all believers," which blurred the lines between the clergy and laity. Even those people who were not following a contemplative calling to the priesthood could have access to God both for forgiveness and for fulfilling some destiny He had for them.

Suddenly laborers and marketplace people could have access to God personally and sense a fulfillment in what they did as a vocation. This came with the rise of the *vocatio activa*, rather than the previously limited *vocatio contemplativa*.[7]

Think about the word vocation. What does it sound like? At its root is the word vocal or voice. Wherever there is a voice or a vocalization, there is a vocalist. If you hear a voice you know there is a person nearby. There is never a vocalization without a vocalist. So behind the vocation is a vocalist.

All of a sudden the concept of a vocation takes on a whole new meaning. It is no longer the impersonal destiny that is defined by jobs or deployments or career. It now becomes an intensely personal matter that connects you with a vocalist who is speaking, vocalizing, inviting you to a path of fulfillment and destiny. Masterful people identify that vocalist as a personal God with whom they have an intimate relationship of dialogue.

Consider the Greek slant on the idea. We often equate the

idea of vocation with a sense of calling. Whenever I ask folks what the difference is between a vocation and a job, they often use the word calling to describe a vocation. *Kaleo* means call. We get the word for church from it. The church is the *ecclesia*— the ones who are called out. Again, when you hear a call of some kind, you always know that there is a caller. Someone is behind that call. It's a person. Behind every call there is a caller.

Suddenly the idea of being called becomes much more personal. It is not simply fulfilling some inanimate destiny for which you were apparently intended as evidenced by your great performance. Now you are in a highly relational and dynamic partnership with a caller who is inviting you to some emphasis, focus, path for your life that provides fulfillment and meaning.

The Vocalist, or the Caller, is a person. We call that person God. God created you. God formed you with the unique mix of abilities, passion, and personality. In crafting you uniquely, then, this Vocalist knows how you will best be fulfilled and experience meaningful work so He vocalizes an invitation. In that vocation you experience dynamic growth, meaning, fulfillment, and find value in what you do—not because of the outcome as much as because of the fact that the Vocalist invited you. Worth derives from the Vocalist, the Caller—God.

Finding Your Calling

PERHAPS ONE OF THE MOST OFTEN ASKED QUESTIONS ESPEcially by young people has to do with how to identify a calling, a vocation. Because vocation is not limited to those who walk with Christ it is important not to limit to Christians the possibility that God does call people into a path of fulfillment. Complete fulfillment, though, is only found in communion with God through Christ. But many who do not have that personal communion may find value in what they do because they find their calling.

I suggest that you may begin to find the seed of your vocation where your passion, abilities, and personality find convergence. God has made you. He's given you a personality—how you approach your surroundings. He's given you abilities—what you do really well. He's given you passion—what you love and what motivates you. Where personality, abilities and passion come into convergence and synergy, you can expect to see the trailhead of your vocation.

At first the "trail" may not be a clearly marked or narrowly defined path. It may be a general sense of direction. However, as you allow yourself to be deployed into jobs that are generally in that direction, you begin to incrementally focus, define, narrow and articulate a more precise sense of calling. As you increasingly refine that vocation you sense increased urgency, motivation, inner compulsion which comes from the fulfillment you find in meaningful work that is consistent with what you feel you were created to do.

Again, though, your work becomes meaningful not because of the result—though that is important as a steward of a call, but because of the value of knowing that the Caller has invited you to this path. And you are fulfilled.

But you ask, "What about the people who have a job but no sense of calling to it? They just do it to make money." Good question. Paul was actually one like that. He didn't make money from his vocation as a missionary. He had a job that was not his vocation. He made tents and sold them. It provided him the income to sustain himself so that he could go on to do what he knew was his vocation.

Of course, it would be nice if our jobs always were an

expression of our vocation. But that may not always be so. Don't become bitter. Don't despair. Don't minimize the job you have. Use it to find how you might fulfill your calling through it.

And at the very least, be thankful that you have a job that provides you with the basic necessities of survival so that you can go on to pursue your vocation elsewhere. It's worth it for the freedom it gives you. Knowing your need for money is met gives your job reason, even if it is not the source of deep meaning in your life. I'm sure Paul was grateful that his tent-making job provided basic income for living in order for him to give his passion, ability, and personality to his vocation.

If your job happens to be in line with or an expression of your vocation, be grateful. Pastors especially should be deeply humbled and thankful that what they receive from the church in salary is given not in compensation for what they do but in order to free them from the distraction of having to sustain themselves so that they can give themselves entirely to the work of study, shepherding, and spiritual care.

How tragic it is when I hear of a pastor who is negotiating his or her way into higher and higher categories of income on some trumped-up premise of personal worthiness that commands a certain level of remuneration. They have it backwards. It is not compensation. It is the effort of the people to free them to do the work of their vocation.

Called to What?

In our whole conversation of vocation and calling, we should also drill down a bit on the levels of call. If it is the Caller that gives meaning to work then a natural question might be "What does the Caller call us to?"

First, God calls everyone—no exceptions—to be disciples.

He is not willing that anyone should perish but rather that everyone would come into eternal life in fellowship with Him. Here the call to discipleship is broad and far reaching. But the response is limited. Some choose to accept that call and others choose to reject it. Accepting it means walking with Jesus on the path of salvation. To recall the image of the river in Ezekiel 47, these people are in the river but perhaps not so far as to be over their heads.

Second, God calls those who are walking with Christ to servanthood. He's asking His family members to put on the same mind that Christ demonstrated when He became a servant through emptying and humbling Himself. That servanthood is a hard path. It is not something that is particularly easy since it requires denial of self and personal surrender. Answering this call often leads to brokenness and suffering. This is the pathway on which we are divested of personal interests and agendas in order to become useful and sensitized to the purposes of God. In embracing servanthood, we find ourselves in the middle of the river where our feet cannot touch; completely surrendered to the flow of God's will. It's an experience of transformation at the deepest levels of our identity.

Third, God at times calls women and men to leadership in His Church. Sometimes called vocational ministry, this term is reminiscent of the earliest references to the contemplative life of reflection, spiritual leadership, shepherding and care. Its precursor is the call that God gave to Levi in the Israelites' exodus from captivity.

Remember when Moses assigned the various tribes of the nation to particular locations in the camp as they made their way across the desert? Each had a place. Levi had none. Levi was assigned to the tent of God and to be among the people. To move throughout the larger camp and go where the need was greatest. Recall also how when the tribes were similarly dispatched to the geographic assignments in the distribution of the Promised Land? Each tribe was given specific instructions and borders. Levi was not. Levi received no land. The tribe of Levi was assigned to the Temple of God, to care for bringing God's presence among the people, to bring the needs of the people into the presence of God. The Levitical priesthood became the model for the calling to vocational ministry.

I like to tell young pastors that when they are called to pastoral ministry they have no home but the Church. Wherever the Head of the Church needs them most, they will go. In the old itinerant ministry of the Methodist church and its derivatives, the itinerancy was at the root of ordination. Pastors were ready to be moved as the need was evident. Roots, place, location were all luxuries that were not part of the calling to spiritual leadership. Any such encumbrances only served to distract the pastor from the primary loyalty to the call of God and the needs of people.

Unfortunately, churches and pastors often try to have it both ways—accommodating the need for spiritual leaders to have permanency, and provide physical ties to a place. Perhaps this may be a contributing factor for loss of vibrancy in many churches where the loyalties of the pastor are divided between the call of God and personal territory.

Fourth, at rare times God may actually call us to a specific location. A place, a job, an organization. Most often God does not call to location. But occasionally He does. Consider the Macedonian call of God to Paul. It was a particular urgency to a particular place and people. Mostly, though, a call centers on the condition of our life, the path of our life and the location is

left to us to decide by using reason and principles of stewardship as to how we may best be deployed for maximum impact.

It is not uncommon in contemporary days to hear someone
say they are called to a particular church or job or even place. I
often wonder if that is the case or if they are redefining the idea
of call to simply mean that their own inner desire is so strong as
to be more than simply an option. They really want this and
they frame the deep inner desire as a call—not from the Caller,
but from their own inner self.

The Head Calls, the Body Confirms

THERE IS GREAT DANGER IN ASSIGNING TO A CALL WHAT IS
simply our own deep wish. Using the idea of call to get our own
way borders on abuse. It is a form of coercion. The pastor says,
I am called to this place. Who's going to argue with that? How
do you refute ongoing incompetence that is shielded under the
umbrella of a call? I wonder how many local churches have
become the victim of an insecure pastor, a bossy lay leader or
some other person who bullies their way around by announcing
that God called them to a position, a job, or an action.

To mitigate that kind of abuse, let me offer a simple but
effective axiom. God calls, but the Church confirms. In other
words, where there is no confirmation by others who are godly
and themselves full of the Master, there is probably no call. Or
at least it is incomplete and should not be acted upon. That is
the nature of both the Body of Christ as well as the standard
posture of a masterful life.

The Head calls but the Body confirms. The Master would
not call someone to something that is at odds with or destructive to others or the greater work of the Kingdom. Furthermore,
a person who is masterful will always walk with a certain

humility that remains open to the insight, influence, and guidance of others. They always wish to confirm that what they believe to be a call is in fact consistent with the principles and nature of the Master.

These people are also so intimate with the Master that they recognize their own responsibility to make choices that are full of the Master's nature and reflect Him well. So they never assert the idea of a call to the level of coercion, or abuse. And they realize that as long as their life is reflective of the Master, they will have the responsibility to make a stewardship choice for deployment.

So masterful living opens you to finding meaning and value in what you do because the Master has called you. But that call is most often a call to a vocation, a condition, and an inner nature that weaves passion, ability, and personality together. Specific choices for deployment consistent with that are the responsibility you assume on the journey.

Scripture to Examine: *Exodus 3*

Theological Idea to Meditate On: *The call of God*

Danger to Avoid: *Authoritarian leadership*

Questions to Ask Yourself:

1. What is God's calling in your life? What are you good at? What are you passionate about? Where does your personality fit?

2. Do you see what you do as valuable? If so, what is the source of that value?

3. How does the knowledge of God's call grant you confidence in what you do?

4. If your job is not your calling, are you still thankful for it as a way to

provide for your needs? What is your calling and how do you live it out?

A Prayer in Response: *"Heavenly Lord, grant me a place to care for my needs and those of my family. Make provision for my daily sustenance. Yet may what I do be at Your calling. And let the voice of Your call be the source by which I measure the worth of my days. Keep my hands busy and may I hear Your call to form my future. Whether mundane or exceptional, may I be confident that it is You that has invited me to expend my life, my time, my energy in this activity. And I will give thanks each day for the provision You grant and the fulfillment that comes from heeding your call."*

Chapter Nine

CURIOUS THINKING

IMAGINE FOR A MOMENT THAT GOD IS THE SOLID COLOR blue. I know it sounds strange, but hang on for a bit and I think it will come clear. God is blue, completely and purely blue. Imagine a large circle colored blue on a whiteboard that represents blueness. That's God. Now, on a continuum of a line extending out to the right, imagine that there are various smaller circles at intervals extending farther away from blueness.

Each of those smaller circles represents a person. And each of those circles becomes less and less blue the farther away from pure blueness they are. (The idea is represented in the less colorful illustration on the following page. Remember, we are using our imagination!) The closest one is mostly blue. The next one is half blue. The next farthest has evident blue but is mostly not blue. And the one that is the farthest from the large blue dot has only a small spot of blue in it. It's hardly visible.

What's the difference among all those circles that represent people? Well, of course, it has to do with proximity to pure blue.

The closer they are the more blue they are. The farther away they are, the less evident the blue is.

"BLUE DOT" DIAGRAM

You see, when God created men and women, He created them in His image. That means that the attributes and likeness of God was put into us. A significant part of that nature is the ability to choose—free will. In exercising that free will, we acted selfishly and created distance between us and God. We became estranged from God.[8] That is the essence of sin, separation from God.

Yet in our distance from God, there remains evidence of God's image in us. It may be hard to see. It may be warped and covered so much that it is unrecognizable. Yet it's there, a small blue dot which is the evidence that people have the image of God in them. Because of that estrangement or distance from God, the blueness becomes less prominent and less descriptive of a person's life.

But somewhere in that warped life, there is a blue dot trying to be seen. Consider the deepest sinner. Somewhere in that person's life there is a remnant of God's image that has been so twisted, warped, and covered by selfishness that it is difficult to see. Yet it is there.

Seeing the Blueness

EVERYONE HAS THE IMAGE OF GOD IMPRINTED UPON THEM. They are worthy of God's grace and the object of His love. That is why God's efforts have always been to reconcile—to bring back into proximity what has become distant through our selfish will.

The pathway back into closer proximity always brings us to a point where we must make a decision about what we will do with the person and work of Jesus Christ. While we may be able to make progress in moving toward blueness by means of what Wesley called prevenient grace, we can never move past a certain point without saving grace through Jesus and the sanctifying grace of transformation.

People can be good and may exhibit godly characteristics while still limiting their progress and proximity to God if they do not exercise faith in Jesus as the way to be fully reconciled to God. That is why the Bible is so clear about the fact that there is one mediator between God and people, the man Jesus.[9]

Masterful people look at other people the way the Master does. They are so full of the Master that no one is off limits to love and grace. And no one is beyond the limits of God's mercy and forgiveness. Masterful people are always on the lookout for blue dots. They love to find them and nurture them into proliferation in another person's life. When they see a blue dot, they rejoice and set about trying to multiply it by nudging that person a bit closer to pure blueness. As that occurs the image becomes more and more restored. And ultimately, when that person comes to the cross, masterful people have been partners with Jesus in wooing them to make a choice of trusting in the work of Jesus for saving grace.

Just as God has imprinted people with His nature, which can be discovered and restored to wholeness, so also God has invested Himself in all of creation. There is a witness to God in all of creation. So as we pursue knowledge of creation, we are able to pursue knowing God. Passion for God translates into curiosity in pursuing knowledge of creation.

Thus, whether the truth we pursue is in a person, or within creation, or within the realm of ideas, it all has God's fingerprints on it and leads us to Him. Curiosity for learning and growing moves us closer to God who is the source of truth.

Masterful people are always hunting for blue dots wherever they go. They are particularly sensitive to other people by exhibiting hospitality and gracious Christianity with an inclusive disposition that does not turn any away. They know that God's nature can be found in many places. So they are constantly curious about things, looking for and hoping to see God in every dimension of life—academic, experiential, environmental, relational. This drives their passion for learning, their openness to discovery, and their vigor in inquiring

Masterful people are not closed to the possibility that God may be found in the least likely places. They know that God has created all things, that He is the source of all, the Lord of all. He is prevenient in that He goes before all things. He is preeminent in that He is above all things. They walk in curiosity; looking, investigating, searching to find God wherever He may be found.

This curious thinking translates into some particular behaviors that characterize masterful people. In their curiosity, they are open to a variety of intellectual disciplines knowing that in their open-minded search they will find truth and all truth comes from God. So in essence they are on a continuous search for God and passionately pursue that search with an insatiable curiosity that comes from a hunger for God.

This kind of thinking is open, not closed. It is investigative, not conclusive. It is inquisitive not declarative. The moment they close their minds they close themselves to the possibility that God may be where they are looking. So they are always curiously embracing new circumstances. They test the limits in hopes of finding new truth. They explore undiscovered fields, areas, and thoughts.

Sometimes this curiosity and penchant for exploration and learning is misunderstood as a lack of faith in an absolute God. On the contrary, it is the highest form of faith and trust in God to assume that wherever their search takes them, God is there. Some tidbit of truth will unveil a new dimension of God who is the source of their passion and drives their curiosity.

This curious thinking also manifests itself in a disposition of openness toward others. In relationships, masterful people ask more and tell less. Masterful people are not closed. They welcome new thoughts and people into the circle of knowing because in that openness they are able to explore and find dimensions of an infinite God who has made Himself known in all of creation—sciences, relationships, creation, faith, the Word.

Searching for Blue Dots

MASTERFUL PEOPLE EMBRACE LIFE AS AN ADVENTURE. THE more they can lean into it, the more they are able to know God. Their demeanor is not harsh or given to curt and terminal attitudes that close off the possibility of learning and knowing God more fully. In the academic sphere, the liberal arts are as much a search for God through the breadth and diversity of learning as they are the pursuit of the various disciplines in answer to life's big questions.

I realize that in contemporary discourse the concept of curiosity has inherent within it the potential for trivial pursuits.[10] Many prefer the concept of wonder as a descriptor. I can live with that. However for those not steeped in and predisposed to reflective thinking and a certain spiritual element, wonder is a bit distant. Many people deal daily with their curiosity but may not consider it wonder. Possessing a disposition of wonder does not necessarily precede finding some element of God's truth. Sometimes we are surprised in the face of our own curiosity to find God in a most unexpected place or way.

The person with only one blue dot—at a distance far away from God—may perhaps curiously embrace some small item and suddenly be confronted with a new insight that may stimulate the blue dot into multiplied growth quite by surprise. Perhaps it's a sudden pang of conscience, an emotion once thought dead, a kind motive swelling up in response to a trivial pursuit. Or maybe it is an arbitrary interest as to why their lust has become so self-centered and warped. Whatever it is, that may lead them a bit closer to discovering God.

On the one hand this may lead Christian leaders and churches to a hands-off approach to ministry assuming that eventually these folks will find some remnant of God in them. Or worse yet, it may give these Christian leaders a false feeling of being absolved of responsibility to actively nurture, search and help the person who is lost on the periphery of God's influence.

The appropriate response is quite the opposite. Knowing that blueness exists within every person compels masterful people to active engagement in seeking those people on the edges. They are motivated by the purposeful heart of love to go and find them; to woo them, nudge them, and encourage them closer and closer to God through the cross. What a powerful motivation for the ministry of reconciliation entrusted to us.[11]

Educational institutions in the Christian tradition struggle daily with an appropriate balance at this point. The question that drives the inner struggle is, "How much should we 'indoctrinate' and how much do we 'explore' in academic freedom?" Academic pursuits for their own sake may lead to complete deconstruction of faith while undermining the pursuit of God as the focal point of curious thinking. Yet curiosity is an attribute that comes from God's image. So in itself there should be no fear of following our curiosity within the parameters of knowing and discovering God's nature in us. Of course that presumes that we believe in a God who can be known; and that is the essence of our faith. When investigation becomes its own god, anchorless and pointless efforts cause breakdown and loss of focus such that intellect serves itself.

Centered Thinking

AN ANALOGY MAY HELP. I WAS TEACHING MY DAUGHTER TO drive a car. "It's time to learn to drive on the freeway," I said one day. We had made many visits to a nearby vacant parking lot and plenty of time on neighborhood streets so she could get experience there. But the freeway was another matter. It petrified her.

We made our way to the nearby entrance ramp for the Interstate 10, or as locals in our area call it, the 10 Freeway. As with many freeway entrances, this one was a clover leaf—a long, sweeping 270 degree curve. I could feel the fear in her as we approached the ramp. She knew that once she got on the ramp there was no turning back. Her grip tightened on the steering wheel, her breathing shallowed, her pallor whitened in fear. Stress levels rose.

As we made our way around the clover leaf entrance ramp I was painfully aware she needed a lot of practice. Yet it was intriguing. The curve actually became a series of straight lines punctuated by an occasional jerk to get away from the outer edge. I couldn't figure out what was going on in her head.

After driving past a few exits I told her it was time to get off the freeway—again, on a clover leaf. She immediately stiffened again. But this time I had an idea. I told her, "As you exit, don't look at the outside edge of the curve. Fix your eyes on the inside edge of the curve and stay close." She tried it. Sure enough, the curve was much smoother and her anxiety levels began to drop.

Fixing our eyes on a thing causes us to be drawn to it. Staying away from the outer edges will be one of the results, but the primary objective is to pursue the central edge and stay close. Masterful people fix their eyes on the inside edge of the curve in pursuit of knowing God and reflecting Christ well. The indoctrination of legalistic boundaries for behavior is not the focal point. It's not the emphasis.

The curve leads to the freeway of a free flow of ideas and discovery. But the emphasis is on the pursuit of truth and God, more than the imposition or indoctrination of behavior or doctrinal precepts.[12]

Masterful people tend to be centered-set more than bounded-set. That is to say, they live their lives with a clear and well-established principled center. Usually that means a deeply passionate commitment to know God and a well formed understanding of Jesus Christ at the center of their lives. The principles of the Kingdom become the values governing their behavior. They are not so concerned about observing the legalistic impositions of the institutional church or their own expectations, although those will doubtless be no issue just as the outside edge of the curve is really no issue for the person who stays close to the inside of the curve.

A bounded-set person may have in their mind a set of behaviors, rules, doctrines, or regulations that to them constitutes holy living. They take great pains to observe, learn, and teach those. Their eyes are focused on the boundaries or limits which define their faith instead of the center which holds it in ordered balance. This bounded person may struggle with fear, trying to stay away from the edges and find that it becomes a difficult and usually legalistic task to do so. Paul speaks of this throughout his writing—especially in Romans 7-8 and in Colossians 2.

And this pattern of bounded, fear-based thinking is not reserved for religious fundamentalists alone. Often a reverse form of this same pattern finds expression in the academy where intellectual prowess is encouraged at all costs, even at the expense of a Christian worldview. In the process there is such bondage to the outer edge of scholarly pursuit under the guise of enlightenment that the principled center is forgotten or ignored out of fear that it will become too confining or restrictive. The result is an environment where anything goes as long as dialogue happens. It becomes a bounded environment in reverse.

In this case, legalism does not mean behaving in a certain way or holding certain doctrinal positions. Legalism is an imposed expectation that real truth requires limitless and uncentered dialogue for its own sake. Many academics pride themselves in divesting their dialogue of any centeredness. They think that is truly liberated thinking. In reality, without the center—especially God who is truth—their exercise in thinking becomes intellectualism for its own sake.

In being a centered-set person, then, the natural consequence is an internal confidence in the principles of Christ that give balance and order to an ever-widening spiral reaching out in curious investigation to learn, grow, and explore their faith. The security of the center gives both confidence and freedom to pursue the edges of thinking new thoughts and exploring new ideas. It informs and provides a framework for investigation such that fear of stepping "out of bounds" is replaced by exhilaration at "stretching to the edges."

To use Wesley's metaphor again, love is the house in which we live. Repentance and justification is the access to it. And the journey of sanctifying grace is the wonderful process of exploring all the rooms of the house with an inbred curiosity that comes from God's image in us and can only be satiated by exploration in pursuit of Him.

Scripture to Examine: *Job 38*

Theological Idea to Meditate On: *The mystery of God*

Danger to Avoid: *Pluralism and relativism*

Questions to Ask Yourself:

1. Where do you see the mysteries of God? Within you? In others? In Creation?

2. Where are your eyes fixed? On the boundaries or the center? How does fixing your eyes on the center free you to explore the big questions of life without fear?

3. What are the questions you most fear asking? Is it possible that God may be there waiting to meet you with new insight?

4. How can you shift your focus from a bounded-set person to centered-set in attempting to pursue the mysteries of God and knowing Him?

A Prayer in Response: *"How wondrous are the mysteries of Your ways, oh God. Though I will never comprehend, I will embrace them. In the greatness of Your being, I take refuge. Yet it compels me to know more. As I ask and explore, my greatest desire is to find You. So Heavenly God, let me find You where I least expect; where I search and explore. Let me revel in the unknowableness of Your mysteries. And may my life be fueled till I die with the passion of pursuing Your being. Help me to inquire; and guide my inquiry that my faith will be strengthened in You."*

Chapter **Ten**

RESTORED SELF

IN OUR LIVING ROOM THERE IS A MIRROR. IT'S ANTIQUE and full length. The mirror is framed in a beautiful wooden stand with four legs and a horizontal axis so that you can tilt it up or down depending on how tall you are. Filigree brass keys tighten the axis to hold the mirror in position so it doesn't tip randomly. The top of the frame in which the mirror is held is carved beautifully with intricate shapes. It is a piece of masterful craftsmanship that is quite valuable and graces the living room with a majestic presence.

If you tilt the mirror just so, there is one place in the middle of the room where you can stand and see yourself—head to foot. An accurate, complete image reflects back at you, useful before going out to an important event. But it has to be oriented to the proper spot in order to give a complete reflection. On occasion, though, especially after cleaning, the brass keys on each side of the mirror loosen and the mirror moves in the frame. Then when I stand in front of the mirror, I can only see a portion of myself—usually my knees and feet! And the rest of what I see is a reflection of something else—the floor and rug. Or if it tips back, I might only see the top of my head and the ceiling or top of the window behind me. Definitely not a full image of the one standing and looking into it.

Once, after all the Christmas decorations had been put away and the furniture in the living room was rearranged to fill the spot where the tree had been, the mirror was crooked. The brass keys had come loose and the whole frame had been moved. It was aimed in the wrong direction toward the wall. When I stood in the middle of the room and looked, I couldn't see anything that even resembled me. It was completely disoriented reflecting the things it was pointed at.

A Full Reflection

WHEN GOD CREATED YOU, IT WAS LIKE HE MADE A MIRROR. When He looked at the mirror, framed by the other elements of His creation, He saw a complete, clear reflection of His own image. Although the frame was good, when He saw the image of Himself on us, God said, "It's very good." Not a narcissistic statement or an egotistical assertion. It was simply a statement of recognition that what He saw was a good reflection of what He truly valued. God's own character of holiness was looking back at Him. That was really good.

But part of that image included the ability to choose—to reach up and loosen the keys and aim the mirror. That free will made it possible for humanity as a whole to decide where it wanted to point itself and determine its own orientation. We decided to orient ourselves away from God. To point ourselves in a different direction by aiming at a different point of reference. Our motive was selfishness and the result is that we naturally reflect other things that gratify or fuel our self importance.

Oh sure, we had some help from someone who really didn't want us focused on God—Satan—but ultimately the choice was ours. And it continues to be each day.

"What is the orientation of my life?" we might ask ourselves. "Is it to the center of the room where God is looking for His reflection again? Is it in some other direction of my own choosing where I reflect a different image?"

I realize that the analogy breaks down at an important point. God's image exists within every person whether they are pointed at God or not. By being turned to a different reference point that image becomes obscured. It is covered by other priorities. It becomes warped and misshapen by the selfish agenda and it needs to be reoriented.

But the reality of God's image reflected by a mirror created and imprinted with God's nature captures the essence of our relation to Him and lays the ground work for understanding more completely God's work of salvation.

You see, salvation is not simply getting a ticket to heaven so you can boycott hell. It is not simply saying the sinner's prayer so your name will be written in the book in heaven. It's not solely the work of paying the penalty for sin. Salvation is much more.

Restoring the Image

WHEN WE RECOGNIZE THE NATURE OF HOW WE WERE CREated in the image of God and are not reflecting that image well, salvation becomes more progressive. When we see that the nature of sin comes from within us and is not simply some external force that is imposed on us, salvation becomes reorienting. When we see that sin is an illness that has caused the image to become warped, salvation becomes healing. When we see the sadness in God's heart when our focus is on something other than Himself in reciprocal love, salvation becomes relational. When we see that the battle ground is not so much external to us in the cosmic landscape but rather within us contending for our will to choose a reference point to reflect, salvation becomes personal.

Salvation is the restoration of the image of God in us. It is progressive beyond the single point of saying the sinner's prayer. It is reorienting as the propensity to tilt toward sinful activity gives way to adjusting your life orientation toward Christ. It is healing in the re-weaving of God's grace into the brokenness of your life causing wholeness that is integrated and healthy. It is relational as the motivating love of God begins to be reflected in deep love that motivates you in relational action toward yourself and others. Salvation is the restoration of the image of God in us.

Admittedly, most of us, if we've been Christians for long, have had pet phrases hammered into our vocabulary and defined in doctrinal terms. Repentance, justification, regeneration, adoption, sanctification—to name a few. There's nothing wrong with these words, unless their doctrinal meaning becomes the litmus test that saves us.[13] Each of these words describes a component of this big concept of full salvation. It's all part of the process of restoring the image of God in us.

For many reasons salvation is most often equated with the single act of "getting saved." That point is when someone accepts Jesus personally into their heart and trusts Christ for their eternal destiny. While that is essential and necessary, it is not the complete picture. Full salvation is reorienting the mirror frontwards. It's tilting the mirror back to how it was made, so that when God stands in the middle of the room and looks, He sees Himself once again. Being restored is more than "getting saved."

REPENTANCE

Being restored begins with what we have described as repentance. That means turning. It means abandoning one focus and turning to another. It's much more than simply turning away from sin, it also includes turning toward God.

I heard Dale Winslow, pastor of a church in California describe repentance with two basic types. When I'm headed east on Interstate 10 from L.A. toward Palm Springs and realize I forgot my wallet, I get off the freeway, cross over on a bridge, and get going the other direction to go back and get my wallet. I repent of going east and start going west.

Something catalytic happens to cause that kind of repentance. Usually it is associated with remembering. Remembering that you forgot your wallet; or remembering that the kind of life you are living is not how you were made or what you were intended for. Something deep inside remembers the imprint that has a higher purpose. We often call that catalytic moment of remembering, conviction. It's when all of a sudden the truth of something comes to the forefront of your mind. You remember and know that you have to do something to correct it. The Holy Spirit of God is constantly trying to awaken that memory. That's grace at work even before you decide. And repentance is when you say, "Yes. I remember my wallet and will do something about it. I will turn from heading east and start going west."

Repentance is the result of inner conviction. I feel convicted that what I'm doing and the condition I am in is not right. So I turn. At the core of that conviction is remembering. In the deep recesses of your being the image imprinted upon you by your Creator stirs and seeks acknowledgement. A quiet awakening begins, as if from a coma of desensitized selfish living. And with the help of the Holy Spirit you turn.

But repentance also happens when you are well on your way back west. When you're in the middle lane of the freeway heading west, you may notice a truck ahead. And you know that you will collide if you keep going. So you choose to shift lanes in order to proceed unobstructed on your way forward. You repent of the middle lane and shift into the fast lane in order to progress unhindered. Repentance continues as a disposition of your life as you proceed forward negotiating the many obstacles in your path. An awakened life heading west may at times make poor choices that result in being stuck in a jam. But with the grace of God that continues to form your life more and more into the image of God, you learn and grow in repenting of things that delay or encumber you on the Free Way.

JUSTIFICATION

This word probably more than any other captures what we most often imagine salvation to be. It is a point in time when something dramatic happens. It is a single moment after which everything is different. Justification is a judicial term. And it is a declaration.

If you stand in a court of law before the judge usually it means you are on trial for some action. The question is whether what you did was justified or not. Arguments are made. But at some point the judge lifts the gavel and drops it with the declaration of guilty or not guilty. In that moment a decision is made and you are either justified or not in what you have done.

You stand exposed in a grand courtroom and God looks at

you to determine your guilt or innocence. When you claim the work of Jesus on your behalf, there is a point where the gavel comes down and in that moment you are declared not guilty. You are said to be justified in your action. Not justified in the action that put you there to begin with, but justified in relying on the work of Christ for you.

This is the point where we see the singularity of the way to being restored in God's image. There is no other defense, no other means, no other argument, no other advocate except the person of Jesus Christ whose work will permit God's gavel to come down with a not guilty verdict. In that moment you are declared to be justified.

REGENERATION

God's grace—or God's presence—has been at work for a long time even before justification, or "getting saved." That's the only way you even have the ability to say yes. It's that grace nudging you and reminding you of how you were made for something more.

But now that you've decided to rely on the work of Christ so you can be justified in front of God, new opportunities open up. Suddenly there is an awakening inside. It's like some new life begins to grow. New interests spark. New desires grow. New ideas take root. The life that was imprinted in you begins to awaken from a deep and long sleep. In reality they are not new at all. They are latent and subverted under the influence of your own selfishness.

What was alive had died when the mirror was pointed somewhere else other than at its source of life. But now as it is being reoriented toward God again, life begins to sparkle. What was dead begins to come alive again. It is regenerating and starting to grow. Passions, interests, abilities, senses, gifts—all engaging as if for the first time with the rest of God's creation. You now start to see things differently and life gradually takes on new meaning. It doesn't mean the consequences of your bad choices before now go away. But it does mean that those consequences can be life-giving in forming new life in you.

ADOPTION

With the new life comes a recognition that it is not given exclusively to only one person. Rather it is life that invites into oneness with the source of life and into interrelationship with others who also are becoming restored. In that respect, then, it's like becoming part of a family.

Of course becoming part of a family also carries with it the responsibility of learning the family values and principles. Getting adopted is easy. It requires some decisions and legal work. There comes a point when the decision is made that you are adopted. The gavel comes down and it's done. But living in the new family is another matter altogether.

The social patterns, relationships, values, priorities, communication, and interdependence all become a lifetime journey of development in the newly adopted person. The hardest part of adoption is not getting adopted, but adjusting to the new family. It has rules and guidelines. There are acceptable patterns of behavior and some that are not. There are actions that are okay and some that are not. Adjusting to those can be a jolting process full of tension and frustration.

Every family has its principles and values. God's family is no exception. Learning those and adjusting your daily life into conformity with those is a long process. The more you practice, the more natural it becomes. In the family of God, those family values are best found in the principles of the Kingdom. That's God's family and His Kingdom has an environment and values that are all its own.

To discover those, you might try glancing through the New Testament. Everywhere you see the words "one another" or "one to another" you will find a family value. As you embrace those family values, you begin to discover that they become second nature to you. And pretty soon you see them not so much as restrictions but as principles that guide your living.

SANCTIFICATION

This whole journey of becoming like Christ as a family member is really part of sanctification. But there comes a point where the primary tilt to the foreign and selfish priority gives way to a primary tilt toward God and His image. The mirror is significantly readjusted and now it's a matter of tuning in to refine and frame the image in greater fullness.

Is it possible to make a mistake and turn the mirror the wrong way? Of course. That possibility always exists. But the magnetic draw is increasingly to the One in the center of the room, not to some other image above your head or in a different direction.

Sanctification is the journey where significant decisions are made by which you let go of your obsession with yourself and other things and are rewired internally to reflect Christ well. Since Christ is the perfect image of God, we follow His model in being restored. In Christ the fullness of God was seen. In Christ we beheld the glory of God. So in sanctification we are being transformed into the likeness of Jesus.

The word sanctification, more than any other, is misunderstood. Perhaps the misunderstanding is because there are so many uses of it in the Bible. Also perhaps it's because we equate it so much with the rules and regulations of a Christian life. But in reality this word is not about restriction. It is not about defining behaviors. It is not about exclusive doctrines. It is not about living up to rules. It is about living beyond the rules, in the unfettered freedom of reflecting the nature and priority of Christ who is the perfect image of God.

Clearly there are many dimensions to a person's life that are affected by not being oriented toward the middle of the room—toward God. It's impossible to reflect His image in you if you are not pointed that direction. Selfish priorities take precedence. Power is misplaced. Life is redefined. Values are warped and twisted. Ambition becomes contaminated. Sin is accommodated. Self is broken. Relationships are unbalanced.

The destructive effect of sin comes from being oriented toward another reference point. It is overcome as you open yourself and relax in the help of the Holy Spirit who will work the reorienting restoration in you. Your part is to surrender and allow God's Spirit to work. It is not passive abdication. It is actively committing to surrender, to be known, to be influenced by the natural effect of God remaking you as He envisioned—fully human.

In sanctification you walk the journey of fine tuning the aim of your life with the Spirit's help so that the fullness of God's image is captured and made real in you. The framing is oriented properly to reflect Christ. The image is being restored.

Scripture to Examine: *Genesis 1:26-28*

Theological Idea to Meditate On: *The image of God*

Danger to Avoid: *Self-help therapy*

Questions to Ask Yourself:

1. Where is my life aimed? Toward the fullness of God or toward another?

2. In what ways does my life reflect the primary reference point to which I am aimed?

3. How may I reorient my life to more perfectly reflect the nature of God?

4. As I take inventory of my life, where am I in appropriating salvation to my life? Have I repented and turned to God? Have I trusted in the advocacy of Christ for my sins? How am I growing in reflecting Christ whose image is on me?

A Prayer in Response:

> What is my life about, O Lord?
>> Is it to strive and achieve?
>>> I think not.
> Is it to speak and to say?
>>> No, surely.
> Is it to direct and design?
>>> Not by your design.
> What is my life about?
>> It seems it is to be—merely to be.
>> Yes, a reflection of the One.
>> To convey the image imprinted on me.
>> Not to control, but to respond.
>> Not to direct, but to model.
> As you bow, O Lord, so I bow,
>> In humble submission to my circumstance
>> And thereby reveal the gem of your Kingdom.
>> Not bound by situation but in contrast.
>> Embracing the events, whatere they be,
>>> and showing forth your image
>>> in whatever circumstance I find.
> As you bow, O Lord, so I bow,
>> and find what my life is about.

CONCLUSION

How do we walk the way of holiness? How do we become Masterful? How do these ten descriptors become a natural part of our lives?

It's a lifelong journey. Certainly there is a start—a moment when we decide that all of who we are is devoted to being all of what God intended. That starting point may be a crisis moment; a catalytic experience associated with a place, a date, and a time. But it opens the door to a dynamic, ongoing relationship that continues to form our lives into the likeness of Christ.

That ongoing formation is not something that is merely up to us to achieve. Diane LeClerc[14] once referred to the way of holy living being like unclogging a pipe to allow for water to flow and do its natural work.

It's not simply a redoubled effort to exercise the spiritual disciplines so that we are spiritually fit. Many people try harder to become like Christ. No, becoming masterful is counter intuitive. Rather than try harder, becoming masterful is reversing the direction of energy. *Not* exerting our own energy to achieve, but releasing our grip on the selfishness that clogs our lives preventing the flow of God's Spirit from doing the natural work of restoration. Agency shifts from us to God. The direction changes from our exertion to His appropriation. This is truly the work of God in us. Yet without our partnership in active surrender, there is no clear path for the

Spirit to form us into fully human people the way God once created us.

At a time when human nature wants to find the solution, the formula, the silver bullet, this reversal of energy and agency is an essential part of understanding God's work of making us Masterful. It is a work of God, not us. It is for all people, not just a few. It is available, not beyond our reach. It is about being human, not super human.

Because this call to masterful living is a call to the effects of God's re-work in us, finding the pathways and channels to facilitate that work is important. Spiritual disciplines certainly strengthen our muscles. But they do not achieve the goal. They are our effort to exercise. The means of grace, however, are God's way of appropriating the daily diet of His holiness into our lives on a consistent and incremental way.[15]

The means of grace are those things that naturally invite a greater element of God into our lives, with the natural effect of restoration. When we take communion, we are declaring the pathways to our life open to the shaping influence of God. When we participate in baptism, we open the once clogged channel to our hearts, and Jesus flows in. When we fast and pray, we lift the barrier to the Spirit to unmask the illusion of our own confidence. When we immerse ourselves in the Word—living and written—we become vulnerable again to the heart of the Master who first conceived of us.

The effect of that free flow of the Master in us is that we become like Him. We are filled with the Master's character and we become Master-full. Our confidence is no longer in ourselves, but in Him. Our security is no longer in our ability to achieve, but in Him. Our energy is no longer sapped by trying to measure up, but we relax. What a freedom we embrace, not by looking at the ten descriptors we've discussed and striving to comply, but by opening the gates of our lives and relaxing in the effective restoration God brings.

Masterful living—it's the destiny you were created for. No matter what the colors, patterns, texture, or frame of your life, you were formed and crafted so that the character, nature and personality of the One who created you can be evident.

END NOTES

CHAPTER 1

[1] The dynamic relationship between who we are and what we do is described more completely using the analogy of the iceberg in my book *The Integrity Factor* (Vancouver: Regent Press, 2006).

CHAPTER 7

[2] A deeper treatment of this concept is found in my book *The Integrity Factor* (Vancouver: Regent Press, 2006), where I use the metaphor of the iceberg to describe the duality of leadership. Our identity is the formative condition (bottom of the iceberg) out of which our activities (top of the iceberg) proceed as a natural reflection. Additional explanation is given in a chapter of *15 Characteristics of Effective Pastors* (Vancouver: Regent Press, 2007), which I wrote with Larry Walkemeyer.

[3] This is a term used by Paul often in reference to himself in relationship to Jesus Christ. It calls to mind the confrontation he had with Christ on the road to Damascus and the ultimate choice he made to serve Christ after his time with Barnabas. God may use extraordinary measures to bring a person to a point of encounter wherein they must deal with the question of whom they will serve. However, God never usurps a person's ability to choose voluntarily.

[4] I describe this process of emptying and humbling in *The Integrity Factor* in the chapter entitled "The Downward Path." It is most clearly evidenced in the life of Jesus Christ as found in Philippians 2:5-11, also

known as the *kenosis* passage. Kenosis means emptying. It is from this reference, then, that we get the image of the Mind of Christ who showed Himself to be a servant to God, not to people. However in being a servant of God, He met the needs of people which were most deeply identified by the need for restoration back into a right relationship with God.

[5] John 1

[6] In the prayer that Jesus prayed in the Garden of Gethsemane, He is struggling to the point of sweating blood. Certainly aversion to what He knew would be a gruesome death was a factor. But also the knowledge that He could avoid this if He simply chose not to submit to the will of the Father. The final surrender that began when Christ first became human was climaxing in this act of atonement. And that surrender was sealed in His death on the cross. This is true death to self so that the will of His master—the Father—could be fulfilled and complete.

CHAPTER 8

[7] Os Guinness expands and describes this differentiated call in his book *Rising to the Call* (Nashville: W Publishing Group, 2003). The sense of calling to the common people gave rise to the inner compulsion to seek a call for which a person was formed. In this, then meaning and value provided the intrinsic motivation for work.

CHAPTER 9

[8] Colossians 1:15-18

[9] 1 Timothy 2:5

[10] Terry Merrick. "Teaching Philosophy: Instilling Pious Wonder or Vicious Curiosity?" *Christian Scholar's Review* 34:4 (Summer 2010), 401-420.

[11] 2 Corinthians 5:18-19

[12] I describe this tendency in thinking patterns in the chapter called "The Clover Leaf Lesson" in my book *Church 2K: Leading Forward* (Indianapolis: Precedent Press, 2008). The bounded-set and centered-set paradigm is also helpful in understanding the motivation for curiosity in masterful people.

CHAPTER 10

[13] Theological or doctrinal propositions may easily become the sum total of one's understanding of salvation. When that happens, the basis of one's own salvation becomes the degree to which that person accepts, agrees, and applies a particular doctrinal precept or position. In its extreme, this can easily lead to a perception that salvation is equivalent to believing certain doctrines or holding certain opinions on major issues. Ultimately an enclave mentality sets in as a result of this narrow view of salvation. I discuss this in greater detail in my book *Church 2K: Leading Forward* (Indianapolis: Precedent Press, 2008).

CONCLUSION

[14] Diane LeClerc in an address to the Holiness Pastors' Day in Portland used the analogy of a clogged drain desperately in need of the remediating work of Drano to allow water to flow naturally as intended. See also her book, *Discovering Christian Holiness.*

[15] *Ibid.*

RESOURCES

The Holiness Manifesto (Grand Rapids, MI: Eerdmans, 2008). Kevin Mannoia and Don Thorsen.

15 Characteristics of Effective Pastors (Ventura, CA: Regal, 2007). Kevin Mannoia and Larry Walkemeyer.

Maximum Faith (Ventura, CA: Metaformation; Glendora, CA: WHC Publications, 2011). George Barna.

Relational Holiness (Kansas City, MO: Beacon Hill, 2005). Thomas Jay Oord and Michael Lodahl.

Readers also are invited to visit www.kevinmannoia.com and www.holinessandunity.org. Note: Two page documents jointly written by WHC leaders are available at www.holinessandunity.org

* *"Fresh Eyes on Holiness"* — Reference document for future study of holiness in the twenty-first century.

* *"Holiness Manifesto"* — Reference document of unity on holy living.

ABOUT THE AUTHOR

KEVIN MANNOIA IS FOUNDER OF THE WESLEYAN HOLINESS Consortium, a national and global movement calling people to holy living. He has served in ministry leadership for over 25 years as a pastor, bishop, police chaplain, radio host, teacher, preacher, husband and father. A former Dean of Theology at Azusa Pacific University and President of the National Association of Evangelicals, Dr. Mannoia at present is Professor of Ministry and serves as the Graduate and Faculty Chaplain at APU.

Raised in Brazil, Mannoia's career has taken him around the nation and the world, but he calls Southern California home. He loves fast cars, science fiction, and rock and roll. But most of all he loves spending time with his wife, Kathleen, and their three children His other books include *The Integrity Factor: A Journey in Leadership Formation*; *Church Planting: The Next Generation*; *Church 2K— Leading Forward*; and *15 Characteristics of Effective Pastors*. More information is at www.KevinMannoia.com.